Fort Riley

Bennet C. Riley was born November 27, 1787, in St. Marys County, Maryland. He was commissioned an ensign of riflemen in the army in January 1813. During the War of 1812 he saw service on the New York border, and following this conflict he served on the western frontier. Here he battled the Arikara Indians in Dakota Territory and served in Colonel Henry Atkinson's Yellowstone Expedition in 1825. In the spring of 1829 Riley was ordered to provide a military escort—the first of its kind—to accompany merchants traveling the Santa Fe Trail. During the following decade Riley saw action in the Black Hawk War (1831–1832) and the Seminole War in Florida. In the campaign against Mexico he commanded the Second Infantry and later a brigade under General David Twiggs, taking part in the capture of Vera Cruz in March 1847. He was breveted a brigadier general for gallantry at Cerro Gordo. Later that summer, at Contreras, he led his brigade in a charge on the rear of the Mexican position, which led to a decisive victory. For this action he was breveted a major general. Following the war he served in Louisiana and Missouri and in late 1848 was made commander of the Department of the Pacific, becoming the military governor of California where he aided in forming the state's constitution. He was promoted to colonel of the First Infantry in January 1850, but illness prevented him from assuming command. He moved to Buffalo, New York, where he died on June 9, 1853. Three weeks later the newly established frontier fort was named for him.

Fort Riley
Citadel of the Frontier West

by William McKale
and William D. Young

Kansas State Historical Society
Topeka, Kansas

THE AUTHORS: William McKale is director of the U.S. Cavalry Museum in Fort Riley, Kansas. He holds a master's degree in American History from Kansas State University and has taught in public schools and for several small colleges. McKale's publications include works on local and military history. A native Kansan, he lives in Wakefield with his wife, Elaine.

William D. Young is a professor of history at Maple Woods Community College, a freelance writer, and a freelance development editor. His published works include *History of the United States Through the Civil War* (1986), *Source Readings in American Government, Second Edition* (1999), and *Living American History: Our Nation's Past Through Its Documents* (2002). Young lives in Lawrence with his wife, Michelle, and sons.

FRONT COVER: *Passing in Review*, Fort Riley, Kansas, 1853–present, by Jerry D. Thomas. Thomas, a nationally acclaimed artist, has made a career of creating wildlife and western art. His original works will appear on the covers of all eight volumes of the Kansas Forts Series. Thomas is a resident of Manhattan, Kansas.

Fort Riley: Citadel of the Frontier West is the sixth volume in the Kansas Forts Series published by the Kansas State Historical Society in cooperation with the Kansas Forts Network.

Additional Works in the Kansas Forts Series:
Fort Scott: Courage and Conflict on the Border
Fort Harker: Defending the Journey West
Fort Hays: Keeping Peace on the Plains
Fort Larned: Guardian of the Santa Fe Trail
Fort Leavenworth: Gateway to the West
Fort Wallace: Sentinel on the Smoky Hill Trail
Fort Dodge: Sentry of the Western Plains

Copyright© 2000 Kansas State Historical Society

Second printing 2003

Library of Congress Card Catalog Number 99-085897

ISBN 0-87726-050-8

Printed by Mennonite Press, Inc., Newton, Kansas

Contents

Foreword

Not since W.F. Pride wrote *The History of Fort Riley* in 1926 has an author presented an overview of the fort in the story of Kansas and the West through World War I. Using recent historical publications, and with original research, William McKale and William D. Young have written a fresh summary of the fort for the same time period. In the last chapter they have updated the story by including a brief summary of the main mission of the post in the years following World War I to the present.

In this highly readable, engaging book the authors trace the origins of the post, the responsibilities and daily regime of the officers and enlisted men who served at the fort, and the engagements in which Fort Riley soldiers were involved. But more than this standard litany of the military that one might expect in a history of a western fort, McKale and Young provide a look at how the army shaped its surrounding social scene and how interactions with its environment shaped army life at the post. The story of Fort Riley is more than fights with Indians on the frontier and battles during the Civil War. These authors show how the post served as a crossroad of exchange between soldiers and Indians; how soldiers shaped the local economy; and how politics, economics, and a changing mission preserved the fort.

McKale and Young's *Fort Riley: Citadel of the Frontier West* is a fine contribution to the Kansas Forts Series. Readers interested in the early history of the state, military affairs, or Indian history will find this an enjoyable read.

James E. Sherow
Associate Professor
Kansas State University

Introduction

Fort Riley was established in 1853 at the confluence of the Smoky Hill and Republican Rivers in north-central Kansas. It was part of a series of forts established by the United States government to protect travelers, commerce, and settlers as they moved across Kansas. Because of its founding date, one year before Kansas became a territory, Fort Riley's history is intimately linked with Kansas's own. In many ways they both mirror the story of life on the Plains during the nineteenth century.

During the days of Bleeding Kansas, Fort Riley's garrison helped restore peace and order for the law-abiding citizens of the territory. Troops from the post patrolled the overland trails, protected railroad construction crews and wagon trains, and participated in many major expeditions against Cheyennes, Arapahos, Kiowas, and Sioux, angered by intruding whites. Engineers from the fort surveyed and mapped routes for trails across Kansas to the goldfields and "promised lands" farther west. The money the government spent to feed and supply the soldiers, the cash paid to civilian workers who repeatedly built and repaired parts of the fort, and the soldiers' payroll spending spurred both the settlement and economic growth of central Kansas.

The story of Fort Riley is also one of a changing United States Army. Given multiple tasks in connections with the frontier, it served those well. But after the Civil War, as the frontier was settled, the army looked to improve its training and professionalism. Fort Riley changed with the army, becoming home to several schools that made the United States Army more efficient and better prepared to meet challenges as the twentieth century approached.

This book is not intended to be a comprehensive examination of the "Frontier Regulars," as noted western historian Robert Utley referred to the United States Army on the Plains. Nor is it intended to be the definitive exploration of the troubled relationships between whites and American Indians. This book is an introductory look at the many different roles Fort Riley assumed in frontier Kansas and how its relationships with neighboring communities and its purpose for existing within the army structure changed as the nineteenth century passed by.

The primary focus of this volume, as with the others in this series, is the frontier period. However, since Fort Riley continues as an active duty army post today, this work also looks at the history of the fort in the twentieth century. Throughout this century and into the twenty first, Fort Riley continues to reflect and carry on the tasks it assumed during its frontier days.

1

The Founding of Fort Riley

To cross from the lush timbered prairies along the Mississippi River to either the sunny Pacific Coast, the fur-trapping regions of the Northwest or the mysterious Spanish Southwest, meant travelers had to advance across the Great Plains and the Rocky Mountains. The Plains region extended from the Rio Grande north to Canada, westward from the bend of the Missouri River to the Rockies. To many nineteenth-century Americans, however, once you reached the bend of the Missouri the word prairie began to mean "desert." This river was the boundary between God's country and the Great American Desert. Military explorers from Zebulon Pike (1810) to Major Stephen Long (1823) disparaged the land of Kansas and its usefulness. Pike referred to the West as a desert. Major Long and his co-author Dr. Edwin James described the West as sterile, a land with no timber and little water, where the soil is poisoned for growing grains or anything except cactus and prairie grass. Only nomads could live in this region. This was, they declared, the Great American Desert.

But trade and ambitious individuals were already crossing the grasslands before 1800. Fur traders were using the plains and the rivers as highways to bring furs to St. Louis. The Santa Fe trade gained momentum after Mexican independence in 1821. Caravans of Conestoga and Pittsburgh wagons, each drawn by teams of eight to twelve oxen or mules and carrying up to seven thousand pounds of woolens, cottons, silks, velvets, and hardware, made the trip across the Kansas prairie. It was eight

Santa Fe trade gained momentum beginning in 1821 as caravans of wagons began traveling miles across the open plains from Independence, Missouri, to Santa Fe.

hundred miles across the open plains, from Independence, Missouri, to Council Grove (in present Kansas) along the Arkansas River to either Bent's Fort or the Cimarron Cutoff and south to Santa Fe. Between 1822 and 1843 the annual value of this commerce reached $130,000, but after 1847 it often came closer to $500,000. The Santa Fe trade played on the ideals of a nation whose western images had been shaped by writers such as James Fenimore Cooper and Washington Irving. What could be more exciting than fighting Indians and wildfires, fording rivers and crossing deserts, shooting buffalo and other wild game?

American Indians utilized this same land, forded the same rivers, traveled similar routes along the rivers. Traders cut pathways across their lands, but did not at first threaten to dispossess them. For the Kiowas, Arapahos, Cheyennes, and Sioux the greatest threat was to their resources: buffalo, grass, and timber. Traders on the Santa Fe, Oregon, and Smoky Hill Trails were but the first wave of newcomers who would use up these resources. These tribes relied on the buffalo for food, clothing, and shelter. Their nomadic life was a sign of their freedom as a people, a people with the right to hunt and cross the prairies unhindered in search of buffalo and their enemies.

Santa Fe traders cut pathways across Indians' homelands threatening their resources, such as the buffalo, and thereby the Indians' very existence.

Other American Indians lived in Kansas because the United States government had placed them there. National authorities from Thomas Jefferson onward advocated removal of all American Indians east of the Mississippi to the Trans-Mississippi West. This land grab was clothed in all sorts of self-righteous justifications, from Jefferson's claim that this would reduce clashes between whites and Indians, thus increasing law and order and reducing both the need for the army and taxes to support it. In 1824 Secretary of War John C. Calhoun argued Indian removal would save native peoples from "demoralizing white influences." By the 1830s removal to the West was part of all treaties, along with solemn assurances that the United States government would guarantee their ownership of these western lands forever. This would end the "Indian problem" in the United States.

To preserve the peace and protect American Indians from deleterious white influences the permanent Indian frontier was created. Provisions were made for a line of forts to mark and guard the frontier, as well as roads surveyed and constructed to run between them. Fort Crawford, Fort Atkinson (in Nebraska, not to be confused with the Fort Atkinson west of present Dodge City, Kansas), Fort Des Moines, Fort

Leavenworth, Fort Gibson, and Fort Smith all marked the frontier. The idea of the permanent Indian frontier was an illusion. The "Indian problem" just moved across the Mississippi, and the so-called permanent frontier failed to separate anything. Traders, trappers, whiskey peddlers, and fortune seekers, both licensed and illegal, flowed across the border.

The frontier also gave way before the forces of Manifest Destiny. The land acquired by arms from Mexico spread the American flag throughout the Southwest and out to the Pacific Coast in California, encouraging trade and settlement beyond that already established through the Santa Fe trade. Settlement of the Oregon question with Great Britain encouraged movement through the Plains to settle Oregon, following the routes of the earlier fur trappers. But the discovery of gold in California breached the frontier line, as gold seekers crossed the formerly forbidding prairie "deserts" to reach the goldfields farther west. Even greater surges of people crossed Kansas following the discovery of gold at Pikes Peak in 1858, and near Boulder, Colorado, in 1859. Strikes of gold and silver near Virginia City, Nevada, increased the exodus across American Indian lands. The pressures of white settlement in Kansas during the 1850s shattered the illusion of the permanent Indian frontier.

This increase in travelers and commerce across the Kansas plains caused new problems for the American Indians who lived and hunted there. Exposed to diseases more frequently than before, tribal numbers were decimated. Trade routes and hunting grounds were disrupted. The game animals they depended on for survival were killed or driven away, eventually including the large herds of buffalo. Faced with such threats to their lives, American Indians confronted the invaders, sometimes to make deals, and other times in armed conflict.

The early history of Fort Riley is closely tied to this movement of people and trade along the Oregon–California and Santa Fe Trails. A number of military posts in Kansas—such as Fort Leavenworth (1827), Fort Scott (1843), and Fort Atkinson (1850)—established at strategic points along these pathways of emigration and commerce had orders to protect settlers and traders who eagerly sought to reap the benefits of Manifest Destiny. Marching along trails that followed river valleys and the high plateaus of the rolling prairie, soldiers attempted to maintain lines of resupply and communication while also offering protection. From these forts the army projected a show of arms in hopes of convincing any foe of the folly of opposing the expansion of the United States. But they were hampered by a Congress that set appropriations

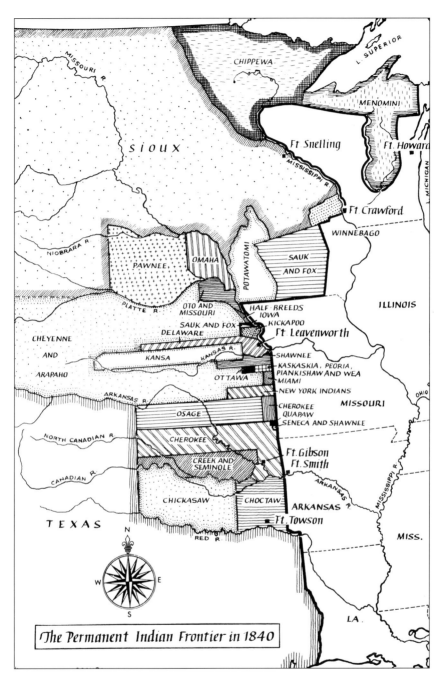

The Permanent Indian Frontier in 1840

To preserve the peace and protect Indians from encroaching whites, the permanent Indian frontier was created and provided with a series of forts to mark and guard the frontier. Sketch from Ralph K. Andrist, The Long Death: The Last Days of the Plains Indians.

and troop strength at levels inadequate to the task. As the army approached the mid-point of the century, it had to reconcile this gap between mission and resources.

The officers and soldiers who served on the frontier were carrying out a mission, as defined by their generation, of protecting the advance of American civilization. They included men of differing opinions about the nation's future course, but they were bonded by a profession of arms. Eventually, their loyalty and bonds of friendship would be called upon and tested. For the moment the soldiers' attention focused on being the vanguard of a people intent upon subduing and domesticating a wilderness.

The most identifiable goal of the frontier army in the 1850s was to convince the Cheyennes, Arapahos, Sioux, Kiowas, and Comanches not to molest the travelers using the roads and trails across the Central Plains. To do this properly, to confront a moving people, required mobility—it required cavalry. General Winfield Scott made that clear in 1850 when he declared "the great extent of our frontiers, and the peculiar character of the service devolving on our troops, render it indispensable that the cavalry element should enter largely into the composition of the army." Expeditions probed into the Plains in 1834 and 1835 aiming to impress or intimidate the Indians. Twice, in 1829 and 1843, military escorts accompanied the Santa Fe caravans on their routes over United States territory.

The frontier army's mission was more than military encounters. When not at war soldiers served as a police force to enforce treaty provisions by American Indians and protect local Indians from troublesome whites. Illegal incursions by white settlers met the other side of the army's two-edged sword. Troops seized the whiskey of peddlers trying to sell to local tribes, as such sales were forbidden by law in 1834. Whites who ignored treaty provisions and settled on reserved lands were to be forced off by patrols as well. The army also served as a mobile labor force. Troops transformed primitive trails into well engineered roads. While done to facilitate movement of men and supplies between posts, the greater effect was to encourage settlement and local economic growth.

To many officers serving in the Department of the West during the early 1850s—the military district that encompassed the yet unorganized territory of Kansas—the difficulty of defending and resupplying remote posts such as Fort Atkinson soon became apparent. Located on the Arkansas River just west of present Dodge City, Fort Atkinson was more than four hundred miles from Fort Leavenworth.

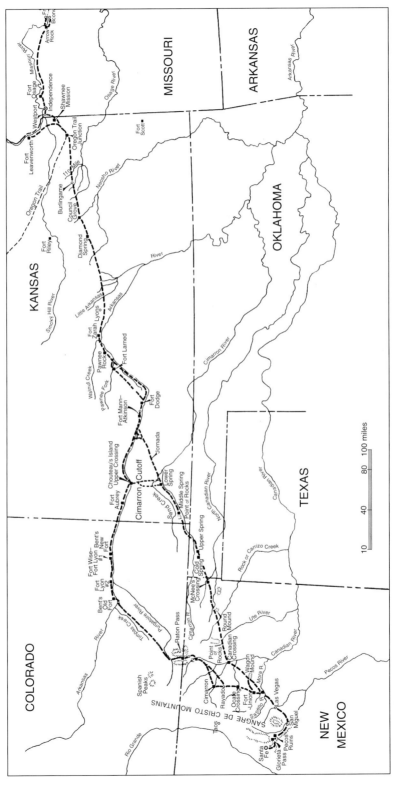

THE SANTA FE TRAIL

To protect travelers on the Santa Fe and the Oregon–California Trails, military forts were scattered along the routes. From these forts soldiers marched along the trails to project a show of arms to ward off any opposing foe. This sketch, Troops Going to Mexico, 1847, *is from Henry Inman's* The Old Santa Fe Trail.

Established in 1850, Fort Atkinson existed as an outpost to protect travelers on the Santa Fe Trail. As the fort could not be reached by water, the army relied upon the traditional mode of transporting troops and supplies: by foot, horse, or oxen and wagon.

The isolation of Fort Atkinson cost the army dearly to supply materials and food to the post, and it incurred a mental toll on soldiers assigned there. This pointed out the need for a more centrally located post west of Fort Leavenworth. Only such a location would allow significant numbers of troops be concentrated quickly, supplied at a reasonable cost, and thus be prepared to complete the army's missions on the frontier. Many army planners and civilians advocated abandoning Fort Atkinson entirely. Thomas Fitzpatrick, an agent for the tribes on the Upper Arkansas and Platte, described Atkinson as "a small insignificant military station, beneath the dignity of the United States, and at the mercy and forbearance of the Indians." This outpost, like most army posts of the period, was constructed from the most readily available building material. In this case, "structures" at the post consisted of native sod covered with poles, canvas, and brush. Soldiers stationed there soon dubbed the outpost "Fort Sod" and later "Fort Sodom."

In July 1851 Colonel Thomas Fauntleroy, commander of the First U.S. Dragoon regiment, argued for the abandonment not only of Fort Atkinson but also Forts Leavenworth and Scott. He urged the concentration of troops at a point "on the Kansas River where the Republican fork unites with it." A fort located at this important river juncture should solve several important strategic considerations: ease of resupply owing to the apparent navigability of the rivers; maintenance of a military presence deep into an unsettled area; and proximity to the Santa Fe and the Oregon Trails. If both the physical structures on the base and the accompanying military reservation were large enough, at least four to six companies of mounted troops could be stationed there. Then strong mounted columns could patrol the major trails each travel season. Fauntleroy also noted the abundance of trees in the river bottoms, and suggested that this land was ripe for development and settlement. He even recommended that the army colonize the military reserve at the fort with farmers and artisans to supply the needs of the future fort.

Such a concentration had been advocated for approximately a decade by other military planners. As early as his annual report to the secretary of war in 1842, General of the Army Winfield Scott called for troops to be posted at strategic positions. He pointed out:

> When at rest, instruction and discipline would be advanced, and each battalion, leaving a small guard behind, might, in column, composed of at least a portion of cavalry, be instructed to make an annual circuit through the nearest Indian country—always seen in a condition to pursue and to strike—in order to overawe hostile machinations and to punish violations of peace.

This plan remained the foundation of the army's frontier policy toward the Indian over the next four decades.

Responding to Fauntleroy's report, Secretary of War Charles Conrad authorized a survey be conducted for the purpose of establishing a fort in this vicinity. In the fall of 1852 a board of officers was appointed and a surveying party organized under the command of Captain Robert Chilton, First U.S. Dragoons. The board of officers included Captains Edmund A. Ogden and Langdon C. Easton of the Quartermaster Department. These men had served on the frontier for several years and were responsible for the logistics of organizing men and materiel needed to build forts. Other members of the party included Captain Robert Chilton of the First Dragoons and Captain Charles Lovell of the Sixth U.S. Infantry. These combat arm veterans brought the strategic perspective of their branches to the selection process. Chilton understood the need to show the flag to American Indians in the region and to be able to respond quickly to any threat. Lovell had experienced the hardships of Fort Atkinson and must have viewed the topography along the Kansas River valley as being more conducive to the establishment of a military post than the high plains along the Arkansas. Another member of the expedition was Lieutenant Israel C. Woodruff of the Topographical Engineers. He had explored central Kansas and the valley of the Kansas River only a few months earlier in anticipation of eventual railroad construction through the area. After surveying the site, the board endorsed Fauntleroy's proposal.

The board submitted its report to Secretary of War Conrad in November 1852. He approved the report on January 7, 1853, and Congress authorized sixty-five thousand dollars for construction of buildings for what was called Camp Center, due to its location near the geographical center of the United States.

2

Building Fort Riley

On May 17, 1853, Captain Charles S. Lovell returned to Camp Center with three companies of the Sixth U.S. Infantry after a hard six days' march from Fort Leavenworth. The troops were accompanied by forty-one "citizen mechanics" employed by the Quartermaster Department to assist with the fort's establishment. This work crew, consisting mostly of masons and carpenters, was hired in Cincinnati and St. Louis for two dollars a day (per person), meals, and housing. Captain Edmund A. Ogden of the Quartermaster Department was in charge of the construction. After establishing camp on high ground overlooking the Kansas River, the work crews built a lime kiln and began quarrying rock north of their temporary camp for the construction of permanent buildings.

Work was slowed from the beginning because of labor shortages. Ogden planned to use at least two hundred soldiers as laborers to assist construction. This was a well established practice in the army, supported by high ranking officials, to maintain soldiers' health in the field. However, during the first two years the garrison averaged only 130 enlisted men and six officers, less than half its recommended strength. Because of other duty requirements only seventy to eighty soldiers could be spared to help. Construction lagged behind, and by November only two company barracks and two sets of officers' quarters were finished. While a few civilians were kept on to work during the winter, by the fall 1854 only two more barracks were completed.

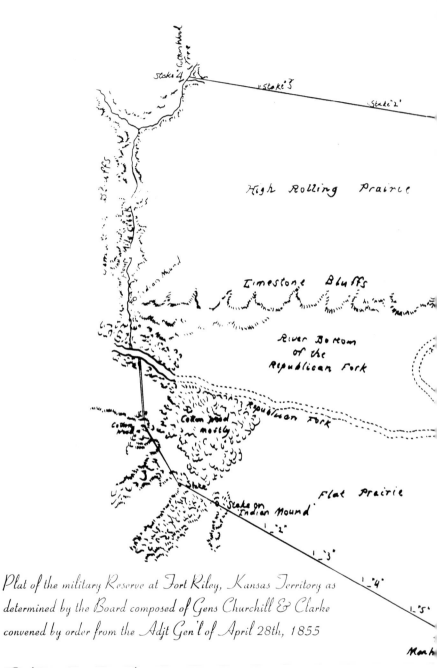

Stake 4

Stake 3

Stake 2

High Rolling Prairie

Limestone Bluffs

River Bottom
of the
Republican Fork

Republican Fork

Coton wood
mostly

Flat Prairie

Stake on
Indian Mound

1 "2"

1 "3"

1 "4"

1 "5"

Plat of the military Reserve at Fort Riley, Kansas Territory as
determined by the Board composed of Gens Churchill & Clarke
convened by order from the Adjt Gen'l of April 28th, 1855

Scale 2 inches to one mile
Surveyed and Drawn May 30th, 31st June 1st & 2d 1855.
Francis T. Bryan Lt. Top. Engrs.

The original boundaries of Fort Riley encompassed 23,500 acres. The fort was located at the junction of the Smoky Hill and Republican Rivers, which formed the Kansas River. The army believed such a location could be easily resupplied by steamboat—a belief that soon proved false.

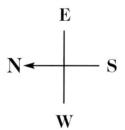

S. Churchill
Ins. gen.. & Bvt Brig Gen

Edmund A. Ogden was born in Oswego County, New York, on February 20, 1811. As a youth Ogden desired to pursue a military career and devote himself to the service of his country. He was appointed to the U.S. Military Academy and earned a commission as an infantry officer in 1827. In the following two decades Ogden served at remote frontier posts from Wisconsin and Illinois to Minnesota and Missouri. He also saw service in the Seminole War and the Canadian border disturbances in the late 1830s. Ogden transferred to the Quartermaster Department and after the Mexican War was stationed on the frontier. In this capacity he oversaw the initial planning and construction efforts at Fort Riley. Ogden, along with approximately seventy other people, died in the cholera epidemic at Fort Riley in the summer of 1855.

As the soldiers and workmen prepared in 1853 to observe the first Fourth of July at this new outpost on the frontier, an army railroad survey team, traveling up the Kansas River valley, camped nearby. They were part of several parties dispatched by the War Department to set a course for a transcontinental rail route—essential to tying the nation together from coast to coast. A member of this party described the day as beginning with a rifle shot at sunrise, followed by numerous firearm discharges. This was the first observance of the nation's birthday in the area. Later, members of the team forded the river and found the soldiers' barracks "in a half-finished state, already making a fine appearance from a distance." Troops living in tents always looked forward to life in permanent barracks.

Four days later the camp received news of Major General Bennet C. Riley's death. A career army officer, he led the first military escort down the Santa Fe Trail. During the Mexican War he served with the Second U.S. Infantry and was recognized for gallantry and meritorious service in the Battle of Cerro Gordo. He attained the brevet rank of major general for his meritorious conduct during the Battle of Contreras in August 1847. On June 27, 1853, by General Order No. 17, Camp Center was renamed Fort Riley in honor of Bennet C. Riley.

The newly named fort took shape on a broad plain overlooking the Kansas River valley. To the north were hills with limestone outcroppings. Across the valley treeless, rolling hills stretched endlessly. The prairie grasses were tall and green from the spring rains and timber was plentiful along the river. From the slowly emerging parade field, the treeless horizons offered spectacular views of this yet unorganized territory. Second Lieutenant Henry Heth, later a Confederate general, remembered his service at the fort:

> the number of wild turkeys in the timber was so numerous that it would appear like exaggeration to attempt to enumerate them. I killed six in half an hour; the combined weight . . . was something under ninety pounds. Before winter set in, quarters sufficient for the soldiers and officers were completed. The chimneys smoked horribly although we had employed the best masons to be had in Cincinnati to do the work. Major Cady (grand old "grandpa" Cady) was in command. Cady was a great theorizer; he worked out a plan, mathematically, for a chimney that was sure to draw well; we were to have no more smoking chimneys. Captain Ned Johnson, who was much of a wag and delighted in teasing Major Cady, covered the top of the chimney with boards; the result can be imagined. . . .
>
> Work was stopped on account of the cold weather, and having little to do, I made up a select party to go on a buffalo hunt. We went up the Smokey Hill Fork five or six days' journey and then struck south, striking Pawnee Fork some ten miles above its mouth, where we found buffalo in abundance.

The hard work building the fort, patriotic celebrations, and buffalo hunts were not the only events occurring the first year of Fort Riley's existence. The symbolic continuity of the army was observed in the form of the first reenlistment at the new fort. This occurred in August 1853 when First Sergeant Isaac Neff, Company H, Sixth Infantry, was sworn in for his second enlistment.

After the busy summer and fall Major Ogden informed the Quartermaster Department of the building accomplishments from the combined efforts of the civilian and soldier work force. He reported in late November the first double block of officers' quarters and barracks ready for occupancy and that the commanding officer had moved into

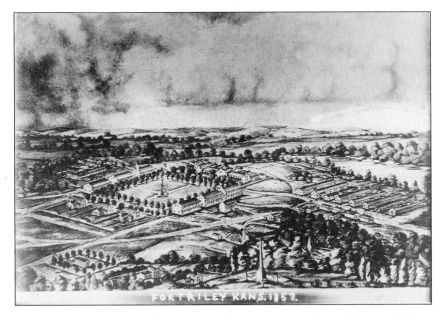

An early 1880s sketch depicting an idealized view of Fort Riley in 1857.

these quarters earlier in the month. Soon to be completed were two more buildings for officers and soldiers "so that although somewhat crowded now the inconvenience will be but temporary." In addition, temporary structures for the hospital and storehouses would be finished shortly. All of this would have to supply sufficient shelter from the coming Kansas winter. Notwithstanding Ogden's optimism, the crude quarters and barracks must have been crowded as post returns for the final three months of 1853 record an average garrison of 10 officers and 203 enlisted men.

This changed in 1855 when Congress and the War Department responded to the perceived threat of American Indian hostilities by ordering Fort Riley be constructed as a cavalry post, increasing its garrison and speeding up construction so the troops could fulfill their missions. Brevet Major Ogden was ordered to "Complete as expeditiously as possible by hired labor, quarters, barracks and stables . . . sufficient for ten companies of dragoons in addition to the two companies of infantry now constituting the garrison." All of the new buildings were to be constructed of stone quarried in the vicinity of Fort Riley, since local timber supplies were limited. To ship timber into Fort Riley would cause delay and add at least 50 percent to construction costs, according to

Percival G. Lowe spent nearly two decades on the frontier, first as a dragoon recruit and soldier and later as a freight master. During the summer of 1855 he worked for a private contractor, transporting supplies to the newly established Fort Riley. That same summer he played an instrumental role in restoring order to the fort during a cholera epidemic. Such accounts of his life on the frontier were published in Five Years a Dragoon ('49 to '54) and Other Adventures on the Great Plains.

Major Ogden's estimates. The firm of Sawyer and McIlvain of Cincinnati was contracted for all the doors, frames, window sashes, and other woodwork. These would be made at its factory in Cincinnati, then loaded with all additional lumber, glass, and hardware onto steamboats to Fort Leavenworth, and then shipped by wagon from Leavenworth to Fort Riley. A larger civilian work force of more than four hundred craftsmen and mechanics was again recruited from Cincinnati and St. Louis and transported by post wagonmaster Percival G. Lowe from Fort Leavenworth to Fort Riley. But Lowe only had sufficient wagons to transfer the workers to the area and then had to return to Leavenworth for the construction supplies. Lowe was forced into extra trips when the water levels of the Kansas River fell too low for navigation upriver as far as Fort Riley.

The failure of river transportation and supply was a great disappointment to Ogden. The selection board chose to locate Fort Riley at the confluence of the Republican and Smoky Hill Rivers to ensure lower transportation and supply costs. Major Ogden predicted the success of water transportation in the fall of 1853, and this prediction seemed confirmed in April 1854. That month the steamer *Excel* ascended the Kansas River to the fort, delivering eleven hundred barrels of flour. More successful trips took place during the spring, prompting a declaration that supplying Fort Riley by water was practicable for "suitable steamers" at least "three months" of the year. The assumption that the river was navigable proved to be one of the first sweeping errors about the reliability of the Kansas River. During the next twelve years, 1854 to 1866, thirty-four steamers attempted to climb the river, but only three made it to Fort Riley. The failure of water transportation meant at least a four-fold increase in supply costs. As a result, the Quartermaster Department called for the construction of a usable military road between Fort Leavenworth and Fort Riley, with all appropriate grading improvements and bridges along the way. These road improvements would promote local settlement and the economy, but they would do little in the short term to solve the financial problem of supplying the fort.

So the lumber, construction supplies, and machinery came to Fort Riley with wagonmaster Lowe's assistance. Ogden tried to anticipate problems and avoid delays by providing the carpenters with a steam-driven Pages Double Portable Sawmill and Patent Shingle Machine. By July 1855 work was in full swing, with excavations for new foundations, quarrying stone, making bricks and lime all advancing at an acceptable pace. This happened without help from soldiers, as most of the garrison was moved to other stations or sent on patrol that summer. By the end of July a sturdier brick, lime, and charcoal kiln replaced the original, and the first new two-story stone building was finished except for hanging the doors. This completed building was appropriated for offices and storage, including the two large iron safes containing the civilian payroll. Most of the workers were living in the original barracks while the rest lived in tents. They were paid half wages at the end of each month, with the balance accumulated for payment when their contracts expired November 15. Their greatest complaints this July concerned their mess because few of the hired cooks knew anything about camp cooking. Nevertheless, with the arrival of the workers Major Ogden believed much could be accomplished before weather forced curtailment of construction in November. In a report written on July 4 Ogden predicted that "unless the parties are visited by cholera or some other disaster," he should be able to accomplish all of the building goals for the year.

Construction was disrupted in late July 1855 with an outbreak of the frontier's greatest killer, cholera. This deadly disease periodically struck and spread quickly, often due to the lack of understanding personal hygiene. Within a week after the first death on July 24 a dozen workers

Philip St. George Cooke, a career army officer, graduated from the U.S. Military Academy in 1827. He served with the Sixth Infantry and accompanied Major Bennet Riley on the first military escort down the Santa Fe Trail in 1829. He transferred to the newly organized First Dragoons in 1833 and later served with and commanded the Second Dragoons. In the fall of 1855 he came to Fort Riley. His years of campaigning on the frontier enabled him to prepare a manual for mounted warfare. Cooke's daughter Flora married the young and dashing cavalry officer James Ewell Brown (J.E.B.) Stuart in November 1855 at Fort Riley.

had died. Major Ogden became ill the morning of August 2 and died shortly after noon on August 3. The disease spread rapidly, killing seventy-five to one hundred others before the epidemic ended one week later. Assistant Surgeon James Simons abandoned the post with his family, adding to the crisis for those remaining. Terrified for their lives, more than 150 workers deserted the fort, many taking military supplies or mules for transportation. A small group broke into the sutler's supplies, arming themselves with whiskey and weapons and threatening violence until they were faced down by wagonmaster Lowe. Confidence returned with the arrival of new commander Captain Washington J. Newton, a new post surgeon, and a new water supply. Until now the fort had taken water directly from the Kansas River south of where the Republican and Smoky Hill Rivers joined. Believing the cloudy, brackish waters of the Smoky Hill River were responsible for disease, the post began drawing supplies only from the "sparkling clear" waters of the Republican.

By September 1, 1855, work was at full speed. Wagons made regular trips to Fort Leavenworth for additional construction supplies, and most civilian workers were transported back east and discharged November 15, as stipulated in their contracts. By December the new post commander, Colonel Philip St. George Cooke of the Second Dragoons, reported construction at Fort Riley was going well. Three new sets of officers' quarters were finished and occupied, with a fourth nearing completion. Five of the two-story stone barracks were occupied, and another would be soon. The cavalry stables were all covered except one. Plans for 1856 included completing another barracks and constructing a stone hospital, guardhouse, and storehouse. For now the 391 men in the six companies of dragoons were living in barracks designed for three companies. But Fort Riley was established, and its stone structures appeared ready to guard the 23,500-acre military reservation for a long time to come.

3

Territorial Conflict

On May 30, 1854, President Franklin Pierce signed the Kansas–Nebraska bill opening two new territories for settlement. Immediately, questions and passions arose about these lands being organized as slave or free territories. The theory of popular sovereignty—letting the people of the territories decide whether they wanted a free or slave state—would be tested in Kansas. Officers and soldiers stationed at Fort Riley would be called upon to police the battleground between these antagonists.

Following passage of the Kansas–Nebraska bill, President Pierce appointed Andrew Reeder of Pennsylvania the first territorial governor of Kansas. Among Reeder's early decisions was to designate a capital for the yet unorganized territory. Not surprisingly, he preferred establishing the capital on a navigable river to ensure the community's prosperity. Reeder believed that the location of Pawnee, on the Kansas River and the Fort Riley military reservation, would not only be on the steamboat route north and west but also on the projected route for the Leavenworth, Pawnee and Western Railroad. He recruited Fort Riley's post commander, Major William Montgomery, to assist him.

Montgomery arrived at Fort Riley in mid-May 1854 and soon began acting more as a land speculator than an army officer. Such behavior was not unusual at frontier posts, where the army acted as a preliminary agent for settlement. Montgomery and many of his fellow officers bought parcels of land for resale to supplement their meager army pay.

Andrew Reeder of Pennsylvania was appointed the first territorial governor of Kansas. One of his first decisions was to designate Pawnee as the location for the first territorial capital, thus linking the capital to Fort Riley.

Montgomery's orders were to survey "a tract of land . . . sufficient . . . to afford all the advantages of timber, fuel, hay and other requisites." Complying with these orders, he established a 180-square-mile reservation—ten miles from north to south and eighteen from east to west from the center of the parade ground's flagpole.

Carving out such a large slice of land for military use reflected a belief spawned during the Mexican War that large military reservations were required on the frontier. Proponents thought that such forts would serve as a base from which to protect overland trails while also encouraging permanent settlements. Settlers, it was believed, would build communities near the military reservation for their own protection and for the economic opportunities of filling government contracts for food and other supplies. Justification for such large tracts being set aside had first been made during President James K. Polk's administration. Polk's secretary of war, William Marcy, advocated sixty-four-thousand-acre reservations as the standard size of new posts in the Trans-Mississippi West. Large reservations were supported by the Quartermaster Department, which hoped the cost of supplying frontier forts could be diminished if food, hay, and other supplies either were grown on the reservation or supplied by civilian contractors from nearby settlements.

Major Montgomery led territorial officials to believe that an area not essential to the army could be set aside at Fort Riley to establish a territorial capital. Since no official plat of the reservation had been drawn and sent to Washington, he saw no problem in permitting such a town within the confines of the reserve. He responded to a letter from "Six Citizens of Kansas" agreeing that a town should be created "to supply the present and prospective commercial wants of the citizen community." Twelve Fort Riley officers, five territorial officials, and eight private citizens created the Pawnee Town Association. Included among its members were Montgomery who served as its president, assistant surgeon William A. Hammond, Post Quartermaster Major Edmund Ogden, and Captain Nathaniel Lyon. Governor Reeder along with Rush Elmore and S.W. Johnston, associate justices of the territorial court, were among the civilian members.

A 320-acre site was surveyed, and lots were sold at ten dollars each. The officers who were members of the association did their part to boost Pawnee Township's future by meeting with the authors of the promotional booklet *A Journey Through Kansas*. The authors praised the beauty and solitude of the fort's location and cited officers who claimed they were so charmed with the location that they planned to make it their home after leaving the army. Furthermore, the authors were informed that the government would sell Fort Riley to settlers once a sufficient number had moved to central Kansas. Such information, intended to spur settlement and make land speculations more valuable, was a common tactic among town developers. Reeder visited the Fort Riley area in October and met with the town company. He was impressed by the area and decided to locate the capital there. However, in doing so, he demanded of the company 160 acres for himself.

Montgomery proceeded to satisfy this demand by securing land from existing tenants. Reeder especially desired the land owned by Thomas Dixon and his three brothers, who were selling whiskey to soldiers. However, these Irish settlers refused to relinquish their legal and proven claim. In December 1854 Montgomery responded by juggling the official survey boundaries.

The first Kansas territorial legislature met at Pawnee in this building in July 1855. Land promoters believed the state capital eventually would be established at this site. The resulting Pawnee Town Association led to the eventual court-martial of Major William Montgomery and the redrawing of the reservations boundaries, which brought an end to the town's brief existence. This structure is now First Territorial Capital State Historic Site.

Captain Nathaniel Lyon was selected as surveyor for establishing the boundaries of the military reservation. Captain Montgomery instructed the survey party to include the Dixon land in the survey by extending the boundaries of the military reservation to Three Mile Creek and thus permit their eviction. After their removal he would change the lines to re-exclude this site and allow Reeder to receive his claim. The survey would also exclude the Pawnee townsite. In early January 1855 the survey was completed. On April 5 Montgomery sent the official plat to Secretary of War Jefferson Davis. He then ordered Lyon to lead soldiers to the Dixon cabins, demolish their limestone structures, and evict the alleged liquor dealers and their families. Lyon reluctantly carried out the order. By early spring the plan seemed to be complete as Reeder declared Pawnee the territorial capital and announced the next territorial legislature would meet there in July. The Pawnee Town Association began recruiting settlers from Pennsylvania and elsewhere to purchase their townsites.

Soon after his arrival at Fort Riley in 1854, post commander Major William Montgomery began acting more as a land speculator than an army officer, buying parcels of land for resale and forming the Pawnee Town Association. Such behavior was not unusual at frontier posts, as officers sought means to augment their meager pay. Montgomery's name is visible at the base of this land sale advertisement.

Nathaniel Lyon served at Fort Riley on two different occasions with the Second U.S. Infantry. From personal relationships to politics, he viewed everything as a contest between right and wrong. His differences with Major William Montgomery contributed to the latter's court-martial while in command of Fort Riley. In the summer of 1861 Lyon led Union forces in the ill-fated Battle of Wilson Creek, in which he lost his life.

But ill-feelings existed between Montgomery and Lyon. Such differences were not uncommon among officers during this period. The ill will between these two had already manifested itself over the harsh discipline Lyon imposed on his soldiers. This had led Montgomery to prefer court-martial charges against Lyon. Now, at this critical juncture, differences again arose over whether an enlisted soldier under Lyon's command could marry: Montgomery said he could not. This incensed Lyon who reacted by performing the ceremony in his quarters. Montgomery responded by arresting Lyon.

Captain Lyon decided it was time to take the upper hand by initiating bold action against Montgomery. Privy to the inner workings of the Pawnee land scheme, Lyon drew up formal charges against Montgomery accusing him of official misconduct in the drawing of the Fort Riley reserve lines. A board of officers was appointed to investigate the creation of the military reservation at Fort Riley and its links to the Pawnee

Association. The plans for Pawnee's existence, and the linking of the Kansas capital to Fort Riley, quickly unraveled.

Reeder's authority to establish the capital's site was questioned by the newly elected territorial legislature. Most of these proslavery advocates struggled to reach Pawnee for the first territorial meeting on July 1–6, 1855. The Kansas River was largely unnavigable again, and the promised railroad was still fiction, which meant days of tiring travel by horse or coach to reach the largely unfinished town. Upon arriving in Pawnee the legislators voted to move the capital closer to the center of proslavery sentiment along the Missouri border, specifically to the Shawnee Methodist Mission near present Kansas City. Secretary of War Davis had received many complaints about the land speculations and other actions of both Reeder and Montgomery, and he passed these along to President Pierce. Evidence exists that Davis despised the antislavery leanings of Reeder, and he suspected Major Montgomery's views as well. Davis may have used his office to destroy both the Pawnee Association and the careers of these two individuals. Reeder had already lost credibility on other points with President Pierce and was dismissed as governor in August. Major Montgomery faced court-martial proceedings at Fort Leavenworth in September. During the trial, actions surfaced that sealed Montgomery's fate. At the hearing the board learned that Secretary of War Davis submitted Montgomery's plat to the president for approval on May 5 but with one major change: he had overturned the plan to exclude the land Montgomery had set aside for the Pawnee townsite and made Three Mile Creek the permanent eastern boundary, thus canceling Pawnee's legal existence. The president approved Davis's revised plat. The court-martial resulted in Montgomery being found guilty of "deceit and falsehood," and he was dismissed from the army.

The final chapter of the ill-fated capital of Pawnee was played out later that fall when residents were given a little more than a month to vacate their claims. They all were evicted because they were now illegally occupying government property. Between early October and December 1855 members of Colonel Philip St. George Cooke's Second Dragoons from Fort Riley dismantled the town's buildings. Some of the materials were used to construct the earliest businesses in nearby Junction City. From his new farm on the edge of Fort Riley, Thomas Dixon eventually prospered, filling supply contracts for hay, firewood, oats, and corn to the fort.

In 1855 the soldiers at the fort were drawn into the unfolding drama between pro- and antislavery elements within Kansas Territory. Idealists

In the 1850s Fort Riley soldiers were drawn into the conflict between proslavery and free-state forces in territorial Kansas. A chain of events, precipitated by the Wakarusa War, eventually required troops to be called out to quiet the trouble spots.

and extremists from across the nation were entering Kansas, determined to direct the territory's future. Their differences of opinion and philosophy were played out by politicians, scoundrels, gunmen, thieves, and honest citizens. The task of Fort Riley's troops remained the same: promoting settlement by keeping the peace and enforcing the laws.

Armed partisans on both sides marched in organized columns and rode in guerrilla bands. Outrages were committed by both sides and by criminal elements hiding behind the ideological struggle. Local observers such as wagonmaster Lowe noted that during the 1850s "many of the raids on individual homes were simply for robbery and plunder, and not for political reasons." Bands of raiders, known as jayhawkers and border ruffians, robbed and killed regardless of their victims' politics. A *New York Tribune* correspondent wrote, "If free-state he was cursed for being a Black Republican; if pro-slavery, he was cursed for being a Border Ruffian; and thus both sides were plundered." The editor of the *Fort Scott Democrat* complained, " It is a soul-sinking sight to see family after family . . . flying from their homes, dragging after them the few effects which robbery may have left them." It was only a matter of time until a shooting war broke out. The murder of freestater Charles W. Dow by slavery advocate Franklin Coleman south of Lawrence in November 1855 set in motion a chain of events that seemed likely to start a war. The resulting confrontation was known as the Wakarusa War.

Called out by territorial governor Wilson Shannon as militia to "enforce the law," fifteen hundred armed slavery advocates, mostly from Missouri, approached Lawrence in November 1855. Discovering he could not control this militia, Governor Shannon wired President Pierce requesting regular army troops to ensure peace and order. Until instructed by either the president or the secretary of war, the troops at both Forts Riley and Leavenworth remained at their posts. Before orders to march arrived, Shannon negotiated a temporary truce between the two armed forces around Lawrence. The Missourians departed, speeded not by national troops but by the depletion of their whisky supplies and a ferocious ice storm on December 8. In February 1856 Secretary of War Davis ordered Colonel Philip St. George Cooke and his Second Dragoons to work with the First Cavalry from Fort Leavenworth. However, Cooke was occupied with a court of inquiry at Fort Laramie, and no troops were dispatched from Fort Riley.

The arrival of spring intensified the crisis. Angry and harsh words between opposing sides became violence in May 1856 when proslavery forces burned free-state buildings and property in Lawrence. Within days abolitionist John Brown and his followers retaliated by murdering five proslavery men along Pottawatomie Creek in Franklin County. As this new round of violence began, Cooke proceeded to the newly designated territorial capital at Lecompton. His command included 134 men, 124 horses, and 1 artillery piece. They covered the ninety-odd miles in two days and reported "no excitement on the road."

Cooke's troops remained in the field near the capital for much of the summer, working with troops from Fort Leavenworth under Colonel Edwin Sumner's command. These commanders managed to keep the territorial powder keg from exploding, often by stationing troops in each pro- or antislavery camp. Troops were posted to Westport, Franklin, and Prairie City as well as Lecompton so they could move quickly to trouble spots and protect the "good citizens of both parties." Mindful of orders and the chain of command, troops from Fort Riley did not respond to all calls for help. Acting governor Daniel Woodson,

Kansas territorial governor John Geary (left), with the assistance of Colonel Philip St. George Cooke and the Second Dragoons, defused a potentially violent situation at Lawrence by convincing a threatening Missouri "militia" to return home and disband. The Second Dragoons returned to Fort Riley, and the following month Governor Geary paid a visit to the post, extending his appreciation to Colonel Cooke and the dragoons for pacifying the territory.

an ardent proslavery advocate, ordered Colonel Cooke to march on Topeka and once there "disarm all the insurrectionists" and level "all their breastworks, forts and fortifications" to the ground. Cooke refused, denying the authority of Woodson to summon his troops. Days later Cooke led six hundred men to the territorial capital of Lecompton to prevent a free-state attack. After talking with the free-state leaders, his troops escorted them from the capital to Lawrence.

The new territorial governor, John Geary, arrived one week later. On September 14, 1856, he learned that three thousand Missourians led by U.S. Senator David Atchison were about to attack Lawrence. Colonel Cooke and the Second Dragoons escorted Governor Geary to Lawrence and then positioned themselves between the opposing forces. Geary convinced the Missouri "militia" to return home and disband. As tempers cooled and outbreaks of violence decreased, most of the Second Dragoons returned to Riley. In late October Governor Geary visited Fort Riley and remained at the post three days before returning to Lecompton. During his visit a reception and ball was given in his honor. Governor Geary extended appreciation to Colonel Cooke for assisting in pacifying the territory and in providing troops.

4

Territorial Frontier Defense

T he proslavery-free state conflict was only one of the problems facing the army during the territorial period. The demanding territorial duties repeatedly would stretch the slender resources of Fort Riley to the breaking point during the 1850s decade.

The opening of the new territory and the overland trails traffic also occupied the attention of Fort Riley's soldiers as they endeavored to keep peace between Indians and whites. During the 1850s the army on the Central Plains faced two essential tasks in its relations with American Indians. One was to convince the Sioux, Cheyennes, Kiowas, and other tribes to allow whites to travel unmolested on the Smoky Hill and Platte River Trails. Whenever possible, hostilities between whites and Indians were to be prevented and peace maintained through a combination of diplomacy and force. Before the establishment of Fort Riley the treaties of Fort Laramie in September 1851 and Fort Atkinson in July 1853 bound the Indian nations to not war with the United States, allow the United States to build roads and forts across Indian country and hunting grounds, and pay for any damages their tribes caused to white travelers. By signing these treaties the Cheyennes, Arapahos, and Kiowas acknowledged white possession of the High Plains from the front ranges of the Rocky Mountains to western Kansas. In return the United States government promised to protect the tribes from their enemies and lawbreaking whites, provide stock, equipment, and even instructors to teach them farming and other skills. The tribes would

The Passage of the "Enabling Act of Kansas Territory" brought many Settlers through the Bor…

receive annuities each year at designated locations. These annuities varied from guns, powder, and lead to blankets, clothing, and even specie currency to allow Indians to make their own purchases. Food was the most common gifts, including coffee, sugar, rice, hard bread, beef, and flour. Annuities reflected a government hope that Indians would wander and hunt less if cared for. This also meant that the soldiers at Fort Riley and other frontier posts were to act as policemen, capturing and punishing criminals who violated treaties. As the 1850s progressed, army commanders began enforcing the policy that if a tribe could not keep its individual members under control, the entire Indian nation should be held responsible and punished. Theoretically, this gave local commanders at Fort Riley and other frontier forts a chance to identify and define the enemy, and it justified the operations of the last part of the decade. It also led to misidentifications and punitive actions against innocent groups of Indians.

Compounding the problem of acting as policemen was the army's other task: preventing whites from breaking the treaties by illegally squatting on Indian lands or trading illegally with reservation tribes. One of the greatest problems here was whites selling alcohol to Indians in violation of the Trade and Intercourse Act of 1834. Even in the days of the permanent Indian frontier whiskey traders slipped into Kansas and violated the specific prohibition to "sell, exchange, barter, give or dispose of any spirituous liquor to an Indian in the Indian country."

As this painting's title states, the passage of the Kansas–Nebraska bill "brought many Settlers through the Border Gateways." Opening the new territory increased Fort Riley's duties as troops were called upon to maintain peace through a combination of diplomacy and force.

The 1847 revision of the Trade and Intercourse Act proscribed harsh federal penalties and allowed Indians to testify against white offenders. The alcohol problem was exacerbated by the organization of Kansas Territory for settlement. Both pro- and antislavery settlers brought alcohol with them and actively used it in trade with local Indians. Early settlers often constructed saloons just outside of reservation lands, and they carried on extensive trade in alcohol when United States government annuities arrived for tribal members. Perry Fuller, field agent for a large Kansas City firm, established his combination consignment store and saloon at Centropolis, just north the Sauk and Fox Reservation during the mid 1850s. Sales and trade went hand in hand with alcohol consumption, despite the objections and threats of local Indian Agent Francis Tymany. It was difficult for the army to catch and prosecute violations of Indian prohibition, and fewer than sixty-five cases were filed between 1855 and 1861. The Kansas territorial legislature hindered enforcement by passing its own dramshop laws, which largely excluded the military from all enforcement of the act, replaced them with local officials, and forbade Indian testimony to juries.

The early years at Fort Riley were largely peaceful, due in part to the fort's location at the easternmost edge of the Plains' buffalo hunting region. This came to an end in August 1854 as post returns instructed frontier post commanders to afford protection to emigrants. This order was a response to an event that occurred that same month on the

Indian hostilities, particularly the Grattan Massacre in 1854, resulted in military action against the Sioux, which involved troops from both Forts Riley and Leavenworth. This 1850s sketch, entitled An Emigrant Train Attacked by Hostile Indians on the Prairie, *is from* Ballou's Pictorial Drawing-Room Companion.

Oregon–California Trail near Fort Laramie. Following Mormon complaints that a Sioux Indian butchered a stray cow, a young and brash brevet second lieutenant, John Grattan of the Second U.S. Infantry, rode from Fort Laramie with a detachment of soldiers. He was confident and determined to teach the Sioux a lesson. He believed he could crush the offending warriors with a handful of infantry and a howitzer. Following an unsuccessful parley, Grattan's command opened fire and was immediately overwhelmed by Indians. Thirty soldiers died in an incident that came to be known as the Grattan Massacre—to that date, the largest loss of life by the army to a single attack by Native Americans. This episode heightened tensions on the overland trails, including increased reports of horse thefts and attacks on stage lines.

Responding to this tragedy, two companies of the Sixth U.S. Infantry marched from Fort Riley to Fort Leavenworth and proceeded up the Missouri and Platte Rivers to Fort Laramie in late September 1854. This departure left only six officers and eighty-two soldiers present for duty and led the post adjutant to record, "The reduced state of the post & the amount of labor & duty to be performed—absolutely requires reinforcements." For all intents, work would not resume until spring.

Secretary of War Davis responded to the Grattan Massacre by preparing a retaliatory expedition against the Sioux. In the early months of 1855 Colonel William S. Harney combined troops from Forts Riley and Leavenworth into a powerful striking force of infantry and cavalry. The white-bearded Harney was a big, powerful man whose personality matched his stature. In late August 1855 he led his expedition out of Fort Kearny, Nebraska. Based on his experience fighting in the Black Hawk and Seminole Wars, Harney believed in fighting before negotiating. As he began the campaign Harney declared, "By God, I'm for battle—no peace." Harney's impressive display of force, combined with the Sioux casualties at the Battle of Blue Water, his taking of captives, the suppression of trade, and the threat to continue operations, forced a temporary peace upon the Northern Plains. While most of Harney's troop concentration was in the north, soldiers of the Sixth Infantry stationed at Fort Riley had marched onto the Plains in the spring to show the flag to Native Americans.

Incidents such as the Grattan Massacre and the expanded mission of protecting the frontier resulted in the creation of two additional mounted regiments: the First and the Second U.S. Cavalries. Combined with the First and Second Dragoons and the regiment of Mounted Riflemen, they increased the army's mobility in patrolling the vast expanse of the nation's frontier. Their formation made completion of structures at Fort Riley even more important. Such a post on the edge of the western settlements, able to quarter mounted troops who were not on roving patrols, would be a tremendous asset.

In May 1857 the garrison joined a major expedition to Utah and conducted patrols on the Western Plains. As spring arrived six companies of the Second Dragoons left Fort Riley for Fort Leavenworth. They joined approximately fifteen hundred officers and men to form a force bound for Utah. It was hoped that their presence would encourage Mormon leader Brigham Young and his followers to obey federal authority. From the outset the expedition experienced problems. During the winter of 1857–1858 the troops' arrival in Utah was delayed by weather and the Mormons' guerrilla tactics. The following spring additional troops were dispatched from Fort Riley, and the expedition eventually succeeded in reaching present Salt Lake City.

Fort Riley's soldiers regularly provided escorts to mail trains and spent the summer in the field protecting the travel and trade routes

Patrol on the Plains *depicts a military escort with travelers and traders on the Santa Fe Trail.*

across the territory that might be threatened by the Cheyennes. In May 1857 troops from Fort Riley joined Colonel Edwin V. Sumner's punitive campaign against the Cheyennes, which was authorized following the success of the Harney campaign against the Sioux. Plagued by incompetent guides, troops and animals often suffered for lack of water. The troops learned first-hand that pony trails were not always adequate for supply wagons, and locating safe river crossings was essential to campaigning on the Plains. One company found itself nearly over run by a buffalo stampede. After weeks on the trail, Sumner's command approached a large Cheyenne encampment on the North Fork of the Solomon River. There his forces met three hundred Cheyennes drawn up for combat. As the opposing forces closed, Sumner did the unexpected and ordered a saber charge. As the battle lines of cavalry and Cheyennes closed, the outnumbered Indians fled and the cavalry broke into individual and group pursuits. Lieutenant James Ewell Brown (J.E.B.) Stuart was shot in the chest while he and four other troopers ran down a single Cheyenne.

Although the army reported killing only nine Cheyennes, their destruction of the abandoned encampment, including the winter supply of dried buffalo meat, clothing, and personal goods, hurt the Cheyennes for some time. The campaign ended as part of the troops were

When gold was discovered at Pikes Peak, Colorado, in 1858, traffic increased across the prairie, further disturbing the buffalo ranges of native tribes. In this Albert Bierstadt photo, a caravan bound for Pikes Peak sets out from St. Joseph, Missouri.

dispatched to join the growing Utah expedition. To staff Fort Riley, six companies of the First Cavalry arrived on post in November 1857 and went into winter quarters.

The normal travel along the Santa Fe Trail continued in the spring of 1858. Additional traffic across the prairie increased when gold was discovered in Colorado. Over the next two years gold seekers traversed the major pathways to the Rockies—the Platte, Republican, Smoky Hill, and the Arkansas River routes—and in the process disturbed the buffalo ranges of the tribes who hunted these areas. Traffic on the Platte River route in 1859–1860 equaled the total from the previous four years. The gold discovery at Pikes Peak made the Smoky Hill River route a heavily traveled artery as well. Stage lines established permanent routes along the Smoky Hill, Solomon, and Republican Rivers in 1859. Traffic also increased on the existing Santa Fe Trail as merchants competed to supply the gold seekers in Colorado. Traffic was not entirely moving westward because thousands of failed gold seekers returned east, further scattering the buffalo. Unhappy and threatened with this increased traffic, Kiowas and Arapahos stepped up their attacks on the western trails.

Soldiers once again protected the Santa Fe Trail. Using Fort Riley as their base, First Cavalry units periodically were dispatched to camp and patrol along the Arkansas River. Reacting to the need for an additional link in the forts network, Captain Edward W. B. Newby, First Cavalry, established a fort—which eventually would become Fort Larned—at Pawnee Fork in September 1859. Newby and his troops returned to Riley in early December. Because of its central location Fort Riley became the supply and base camp for other frontier forts. Fort Larned received four thousand rations and nine hundred bushels of corn from Fort Riley's commissary in November 1859. These rations, each being one man's food for one day, were to feed the Fort Larned garrison for months because it could not locally supply itself. The high cost of supplying the new forts meant that most summer campaigners left their scattered posts and returned to Fort Riley for the winter.

By 1860 the passage of mails over the Santa Fe Trail were relatively safe. But continued Indians attacks on travelers caused the War Department to order mounted units to conduct a campaign against the Kiowas and Comanches "as early in the spring as the grass will permit." Consequently, in May 1860 four companies of the First Cavalry from Fort Riley joined two companies of Second Dragoons from Fort Kearny, Nebraska, to conduct operations against the Indians.

The summer expedition of 1860 was the most comprehensive yet directed at the Plains tribes along the Santa Fe Trail, but it concluded with mixed results. Major John Sedgwick led the Riley column in an exhausting and profitless scout south of the Arkansas River to the Antelope Hills. Lieutenant J.E.B. Stuart's personal diary records meals of "a fine roast of buffalo," wildlife including "bird serenade at night," but regrettably "no Indians." In July the column reached the foot of the Rockies. Near Bent's Fort, Captain William Steele and Lieutenant Stuart skirmished with a small party of Kiowas on July 11, killing two men and

James Ewell Brown (J.E.B.) Stuart was assigned to Fort Riley on several occasions during the 1850s as a member of the First U.S. Cavalry. His duties included the usual functions of a young lieutenant, from the routine of garrison duty to patrolling and protecting the overland mail routes. His memories of Fort Riley included his courting and marrying Flora Cooke, daughter of Philip St. George Cooke.

capturing sixteen women and children. But this was the only combat for Sedgwick's command. Although his soldiers failed to locate and punish the Indians, their presence eased the threat. By August the troops returned to Fort Riley. Lieutenant Stuart led a column out of Fort Riley again in September to "display the flag." His four companies of cavalry and two of infantry marched 387 miles west to establish Fort Wise on the Arkansas River.

All of this activity by Fort Riley's troops—whether it was active campaigning, construction, or just meeting daily supply needs—promoted settlement nearby the fort and around central Kansas. To facilitate supply and improve transportation the army built roads connecting Forts Leavenworth and Riley, and connecting Fort Riley with the nearby communities of Manhattan and Junction City. Government contracts went to civilians to build bridges over the Kansas, Republican, and Smoky Hill Rivers. Wagons heading west for the Colorado gold rush assembled at Fort Riley or nearby Junction City for safety, and then followed trails surveyed by the military west to Pikes Peak. The Pikes Peak Stagecoach Company, established in 1859, made sure to include a station stop at Fort Riley. At this time eastern Colorado was still part of Kansas Territory, and civilians encouraged all road building as a means of connecting the eastern and western settlements of Kansas. Communities raised funds to build a better wagon road between Manhattan and Denver, following the road and bridges marked by the army. These transportation improvements helped civilian settlement as well as military supply.

Fort Riley promoted settlement and cemented its ties with nearby communities through government purchases. Federal money and contracts for corn, hay, and other supplies built the local economy and created the local economic elite. The Quartermaster Department, concerned by rising costs, encouraged local interests to bid on supply contracts, believing that local suppliers would reduce transportation costs. By 1857 settlement was dense enough that local residents won their first supply contract. Robert Wilson, the post sutler at Fort Riley, contracted to supply six hundred tons of hay, cut on the military reservation.

By the end of 1860 and the Kansas territorial period, Fort Riley's frontier duties would be overshadowed by national events in the East; the coming of the Civil War would not change the roles assigned to the fort, but it would add to its responsibilities.

5

The Civil War Years

News of the shelling of Fort Sumter in Charleston Harbor, South Carolina, arrived at Fort Riley on April 17, 1861. Feelings of both foreboding and patriotic zeal greeted the announcement. A resident of the fort, Charles Francis Clarke, prophetically recorded the next day: "now we are at the commencement of a civil war which will no doubt spread over the whole Country." In the broadest perspective of national planners during the Civil War, Kansas would be one of the war's largest and least important military theaters. But to Kansas residents this was a continuation of the pre-war struggles: freedom to determine their state's future, freedom to settle and create a prosperous future, and freedom from armed terrorists from Missouri. Geographical factors, such as sparse settlement and slow communication, dominated military planning and preparation. State politicians and district military commanders worked to keep neighboring Missouri in the Union and to monitor settlements and the traffic utilizing the overland trails. Fort Riley would continue to serve as an important outpost to protect settlers and trails. At the same time, its troops would combat threats by Confederate forces, guerrillas, and bushwhackers. These overlapping issues spurred Kansans and the military to constantly consider military preparedness.

The westward movement continued throughout the Civil War years, spurred by mineral discoveries in the Rockies. The Overland Mail Company, a stage service established prior to the Civil War that followed a southern route across the West to California, moved its routes farther north, and leading stagecoach operator Ben Holladay established regular stage lines between Leavenworth and Santa Fe, and from Leavenworth to Denver along the Smoky Hill River. The result was increased friction between Indians and settlers, even as regular army troops were withdrawn from frontier posts to participate in the Civil War. President Abraham Lincoln's administration recognized the importance of westward trails as the gold and silver coming from Colorado mines were vital to the Northern war effort. To keep the West loyal to the North, the army's traditional role—maintaining the peace and safety of the frontier—must be continued throughout the national struggle.

When Kansas entered the Union on January 29, 1861, Captain Henry Wessells was Fort Riley's commanding officer. A hardened veteran of the frontier army, Wessells had served with the Second U.S. Infantry for nearly three decades. He must have viewed the impending conflict as a possible avenue for promotion. Fellow officer and West Pointer, First Lieutenant James G. Martin, was also present at the post when news of the war arrived. Martin, originally commissioned as an artillery officer, transferred to the Quartermaster Department following the Mexican War in which he suffered a wound that resulted in the amputation of one arm. In the past year he had served at Fort Riley, attending to supplying troops.

While politicians in Washington attempted and failed to bring about compromise and end the war, the day-to-day routine of soldiering continued. Wessells and Martin temporarily were joined by Captains William Steele, James M. Hawes, and Second Lieutenant Solomon Williams (Second Dragoons); First Lieutenant James Deshler and Second Lieutenant Albert V. Colburn (First Cavalry); and Second Lieutenant Albert M. Powell (Tenth Infantry). These officers were passing through on their way to other stations and assignments. After evening mess they had opportunities to discuss events happening in Washington and to consider their future courses of action. Eventually, in a scenario replayed in scattered posts across the nation, Steele, Hawes, Deshler, and Williams chose to resign their commissions and join the Confederacy. Martin too, would find reasons to side with the South and defend his native North Carolina. Unlike the officer corps, however, most enlisted men in the regular army remained loyal to their oaths and the Union.

On January 29 three companies of dragoons under Captain Steele's command marched from Fort Riley to Fort Leavenworth for the eventual reuniting of the regiment. Regular army units that had not served together since the Mexican War marched east to combat the rebellion. They would be replaced by new units of Kansas volunteers. This change

Captain Henry W. Wessells, Second U.S. Infantry, was Fort Riley's commanding officer in 1859 and again in 1861. Wessells had served with the Second Infantry for nearly three decades, and when the Civil War commenced he remained loyal to the U.S. government, fighting for the Union with the Second Infantry in the East.

Captain William Steele was at Fort Riley briefly in 1861, and on January 29 three companies of dragoons under Steele's command left the post, marching to Fort Leavenworth and points east to participate in the ensuing Civil War. Captain Steele later would resign his commission and join the Confederacy.

was not limited to fighting men. The regular army surgeon also left Fort Riley with the troops, and Junction City physician Frederick Drew signed a contract to serve as acting assistant surgeon at Fort Riley for the duration of the Civil War. At this time Fort Riley was still on the extreme western edge of settlement in Kansas. The fort's pre-war role as a link in frontier defenses continued, as evidenced by the departure of Lieutenants Deshler and Powell and their commands on February 8 for Fort Wise, Colorado Territory.

President Lincoln's call to arms in April 1861 to suppress the insurrection brought an immediate response from Kansans. In Washington, Kansas senator James H. Lane enlisted more than one hundred men in a military group known as the Frontier Guard. Kansas governor Charles Robinson called for the organization of militia to repel any invasions from Missouri. Volunteers in the nearby settlements of Junction City and Manhattan rallied to the flag and formed the Home Guard Regiment. Along with others, these citizen-soldiers were soon organized into the Sixth Kansas Cavalry. Their goal, according to a local correspondent was, "The suppression of this demon-contrived rebellion; the restoration of peace and the salvation of our government." They soon were deployed at Fort Scott to assist in maintaining order along the border.

The difficulty of keeping Missouri in the Union increased during the summer of 1861, as Confederate sympathizers marshaled their forces to gain control of this key border state. Near St. Louis, Union troops under command of newly promoted Brigadier General Nathaniel Lyon captured a camp of Missouri militia suspected of treasonable intentions. Lyon's troops and civilians exchanged gunfire, and the resulting bloodshed heightened tensions in the state. Former Missouri governor and Mexican War general Sterling Price mobilized a State Guard against Union forces within Missouri. As efforts to avert armed conflict failed, Lyon moved toward the state capital, Jefferson City. Pro-Confederate forces gathered there retreated to the southwest corner of the state in hopes of obtaining assistance from Confederate forces in Arkansas. Lyon and his forces followed, finally clashing with the numerically superior Confederate forces near Springfield, Missouri, on August 10. The Confederate victory at Wilson's Creek cost Lyon his life and returned much of the state to Confederate control. His bold actions however, thwarted efforts to bring Missouri into the Confederacy in 1861.

Many of the Kansas volunteer units who fought for Lyon in Missouri returned to Fort Riley that autumn. They were welcomed back with a reception, dance, and supper. The volunteer's arrival signaled an

Following the Battle of Wilson's Creek, in which Brigadier General Nathaniel Lyon was killed, most Kansas units returned to Fort Riley in the autumn of 1861 where they were welcomed back with a reception, dance, and supper. This painting of the Wilson's Creek conflict appears in the 1899 Official and Illustrated War Record.

impending change of station for the last two companies of the Second U.S. Infantry stationed at Fort Riley. The following week these regular soldiers departed for Fort Leavenworth and service in the East.

The departure of Wessells and the Second U.S. Infantry marked a change in the officers and soldiers assigned to Fort Riley. No longer would U.S. Army regulars garrison the post. Throughout the Civil War Fort Riley's garrison would consist of volunteer regiments, mostly from Kansas but also from Colorado, Indiana, and Iowa. These volunteers, both cavalry and infantry, signed up for three years of service, and filled the bulk of Union armies in all wartime theaters. According to the Act to Authorize the Enlargement of Volunteers, July 22, 1861, creating a national volunteer army, states would raise the men and organize the regiments. The governor would commission field and staff officers and have some control over the regiments until they were called into federal service. The mission of protecting the frontier now fell to a different breed of soldiers. Fort Riley's role as a staging point to protect westward trails and settlements would continue. But the volunteer soldiers were different from the regulars who preceded them in Kansas. The volunteers were often younger and more physically fit, and certainly greater in number than the pre-war army had ever imagined. They held harsher attitudes toward Plains Indians, not tempered by any grand vision of the national government. These troops had no preference for peaceful solutions nor did they feel the need to teach and "civilize" the American Indians. Instead they were fired by a desire to remove all perceived obstacles to the spread of "American Civilization" and their own personal success. The only way to solve the "Indian problem" as they saw it was to eliminate the cause—the Indians.

Similar simplicity focused their attitudes on fighting the Civil War. Their general beliefs were that the South, proslavery advocates, and Missourian's were all evil, and evil must be eradicated. Kansas volunteers believed the regular army had been too soft on Southerners before the war. Once war started Kansas would be cut off from the rest of the Union and open to invasion by Missourians, who Kansas expected would be out for revenge. Isolated, Kansas must be ready militarily and be willing to take any action. These attitudes hardened after Confederate raids on Humboldt and Gardner in September 1861 where houses, stores, and mills were put to the torch. General James H. Lane's Kansas troops retaliated by raiding Osceola, Missouri, on September 23, robbing the bank, stealing goods, and burning the town. Charles R. Jennison's Seventh Kansas Cavalry would become notorious for this type of "jayhawking." These raids fueled a growing spiral of attack and revenge. Kansans and Missourians demanded that each outrage be met with even greater violence. Until hostilities ceased between North and South, soldiers at Fort Riley and other frontier forts added to their other duties the thankless task of preventing or responding to these "outrages."

As 1862 began, the garrison comprised two companies from the Sixth and Eighth Kansas volunteers. During the first quarter of the year, the average monthly troop strength stood at 157. The quality of these and other volunteer soldiers was questioned in a regular army quartermaster's report:

> The regimental and company commanders knew nothing of their duties and apparently had never made returns or reports of any kind. The regiments appeared in worse condition than they could possibly have been during the first week of their enlistment, their camps being little better than pig-pens, officers and men sleeping and messing together; furloughs in immense numbers being granted, or, where not granted,

Various regiments from Kansas and other states were garrisoned at Fort Riley during the Civil War. Above are members of Charles Jennison's Seventh Kansas Cavalry, and below are members of the Eighth Kansas Infantry, Company E.

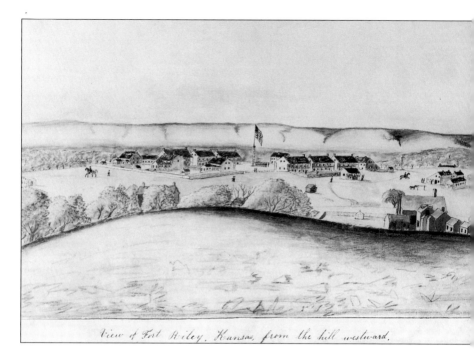

View of Fort Riley, Kansas, from the hill westward.

taken; drill having been abandoned almost wholly, and the men constituting a mere ragged, half-armed, diseased, and mutinous rabble, taking
votes as to whether any troublesome or distasteful order should be
obeyed or defied.

Nevertheless, soldiers at the fort quickly responded to reports of troubles
in outlying settlements. In February 1862 a detachment of cavalry traveled up to the Solomon River to investigate reported "depredations"
committed by Pawnees. They soon returned without finding evidence of
any wrongdoing. Reports came in during the year of Kiowas and
Arapahos raiding wagon trains and exacting tribute from travelers.
The Overland Mail Company route was suspended for part of the year.
These events heightened fears already rampant from news of the Great
Sioux uprising in Minnesota.

The Kansas volunteers at Fort Riley might not always demonstrate
proper drill and regulations, but they did exhibit a sense of knowing what
they were fighting for. This included a strong dislike of individuals whose
views were considered "sesesch," or pro-Southern, whether they were in
uniform or not. In early March 1862 a mob of Fort Riley soldiers concluded that the *Kansas Frontier*, published in nearby Junction City, was
an organ for dispensing anti-Union sentiment. Members of Company F,

This 1862 watercolor by John Gaddis is one of the earliest known images of Fort Riley. Private Gaddis was a member of the Twelfth Wisconsin Infantry, which came to Fort Riley in the spring of 1862 as part of an anticipated campaign to the Southwest. From the limestone outcroppings northwest of the main post, Gaddis sketched the buildings and grounds of the frontier fort. The familiar arrangement of officers' quarters, barracks, and support buildings organized around a central parade ground would be the general appearance of the fort for the next three decades.

Sixth Kansas Cavalry and Company C, Eighth Kansas Infantry "visited" the newspaper one evening and wreaked considerable damage upon the premises, breaking windows, destroying furniture, smashing the presses, and scattering the type. A passerby was killed by a stray bullet during the riotous behavior. Several days later they returned and this time demolished the site. George W. Martin, editor of the rival *Smoky Hill Republican Union*, praised the enthusiasm of the Kansas volunteers at Fort Riley and only mourned the loss of an excellent printing press. Such violent incidents also occurred at Fort Leavenworth and other Kansas towns.

During the spring, elements of the Twelfth and Thirteenth Wisconsin arrived on post. These regiments, organized the preceding fall, were part of a proposed expedition into New Mexico. Once again Fort Riley offered a central strategic point where units could be assembled, trained, and deployed. James W. Denver, former Kansas territorial governor and now brigadier general of volunteers, described Fort Riley as the "most convenient post in Kansas for outfitting a large expedition." But before the expedition could begin, the operation was abandoned. Strategic considerations changed following the Union victory at Glori-etta Pass, New Mexico Territory, in late March. In addition,

Union commanders in the western theater were redirecting their forces to support General Ulysses Grant's army as he pushed up the Tennessee River toward Shiloh. General Henry W. Halleck, commander of the Department of the Mississippi, which included Kansas, believed that Kansas was not an active theater of the Civil War and wanted to move Kansas volunteer regiments "where they might be of some use."

In early June 1862 the First Colorado Volunteers arrived at Fort Riley with approximately 130 Confederate prisoners captured at Santa Fe, Albuquerque, and Apache Pass in New Mexico. They were described as "perfect ragamuffins" and belonged to the Second, Fourth, Fifth, and Seventh Texas Mounted Volunteers. Of these, about one hundred were paroled at Fort Riley and released. The rest remained under guard during their three-week stay at the fort and were put to work policing the grounds, cutting grass, and cleaning the walks. By the end of the month the final thirty prisoners were sent on to Fort Leavenworth under a twenty-man escort.

Captain Daniel Whittenhall, nephew of the late General Lyon, commanded the post for a brief period during the prisoners' confinement. But he soon led troops to strengthen the garrisons at Forts Larned, Lyon, and Union. Other orders sent a company of cavalry to the Saline Fork of the Smoky Hill to search for a group of armed men reported to be horse thieves. In early September, yet another company of soldiers left for Fort Scott in response to another rumored threat of a Confederate invasion from Indian Territory.

Operations did not completely cease with the onset of winter. On December 10, 1862, Captain Horatio N. F. Read left with sixty men and ten days' provisions, traveling up the Republican River. About sixty miles from the fort, he encountered a number of families who had taken refuge with a local farmer. They gathered there because of Indian attacks upon their farms. Upon entering present Cloud and Republic Counties, Read found crops and houses burned and the settlements around Lake Sibley and White Rock abandoned.

While these observations caused alarm, the expedition also afforded Captain Read an opportunity to report on the prospects of future settlement in the area. He reported that the country was very fertile and capable of sustaining a dense population. Even in the midst of the Civil War the line of settlement continued westward. The Junction City *Union* reported in the spring of 1863 that the "discernible frontier line" already extended eighty miles west of Fort Riley.

Captain Henry Booth was placed in command of a militia raised at Fort Riley, which formed Company L of the Eleventh Kansas.

Members of the Eleventh Kansas Cavalry.

Upon Read's return, Captain James L. Stewart reported to departmental headquarters at Fort Leavenworth. He warned that decreasing troop strength at Fort Riley would prevent him from affording protection to settlers in outlying areas. Stewart again sent troops up the Republican River valley with orders to protect settlers. Throughout the spring of 1863 detachments regularly patrolled the river valley. In March one of the patrols fought a band of Pawnees, reporting ten Indians and two soldiers killed. Fears and rumors of Indian uprisings abounded, but the threat did not materialize near the fort or in northern Kansas.

While scouting parties and incidents such as these occupied the post's attention, traders and travelers crossing the Santa Fe Trail earlier in the spring reported that Indian tribes were increasingly hostile. In April, Fort Larned reported a large number of Texans and Indians marching toward the fort. Responding to this, a company of the Ninth Kansas Cavalry was dispatched from Fort Riley to Fort Larned. The approaching Indians were coming to collect their annuities, and no major outbreaks of violence occurred in 1863.

Officers and soldiers continued rotating through Fort Riley to other stations. On July 4 troops of the Eleventh Kansas Cavalry arrived under the command of Captain Edmund G. Ross. A detachment of the Ninth Kansas Cavalry was ordered to Kansas City while small patrols went to the "distant frontier settlements" in search of thieves and stolen stock. Another expedition traveled up the Smoky Hill River to locate stolen horses. Part of the command rode into western Kansas to show a presence along the Santa Fe Trail and convince Indians in that area to remain peaceful.

Still giving priorities to other theaters, the War Department stripped the Department of Missouri of all but twenty-three thousand men, sending the rest to Mississippi and Tennessee. Political infighting between General James H. Lane and Kansas governor Thomas Carney prevented the raising of a special Kansas Border Guard regiment. This manpower shortage and lack of preparation allowed William Quantrill to lead his band of Confederate guerrillas into Kansas in August 1863, sacking Lawrence and killing approximately 150 men and boys. Quantrill's raid caused a general alarm throughout the state. Secretary of War Edwin M. Stanton and General John M. Schofield ordered more than eight thousand stand of arms shipped to Kansas to be dispensed along with cavalry mounts to Kansas militia units. Fort Riley acted as a conduit for dispensing arms, including the issue of eighty muskets from the post arsenal to the citizens of Manhattan. These and other hastily raised mili-

On July 4, 1863, troops of the Eleventh Kansas Cavalry arrived at Fort Riley under the command of Captain Edmund G. Ross, later a U.S. senator from Kansas.

tia were placed under the command of Captain Henry Booth and formed Company L of the Eleventh Kansas Cavalry. Their presence provided some reassurance to settlers in the fort's immediate vicinity. Besides arming the new militia units, troops from Fort Riley were ordered out to prevent retaliatory raids across the Missouri border.

In the spring of 1864 the army created a new military district, the District of the Upper Arkansas, headquartered at Fort Riley. General James Blunt, a prominent Kansan with little military talent and a knack for meddling in politics, took command of this vast military district. The designation of Fort Riley as district headquarters caused an increase in the number of civilians employed on the post, who assisted receiving and forwarding the rising volume of supplies to other forts. By November 1864 this work force grew to nearly seventy men and included carpenters, masons, quarrymen, plasterers, and painters. The payroll amounted to more than three thousand dollars per month. The employees set to work repairing work areas, barracks, and quarters that had not received much attention since the last flurry of maintenance in 1857. Additional teamsters, herders, and wood choppers replaced these builders after completion of repair work. The total number of civilian employees at Fort Riley did not decrease until the following summer.

Before the spring thaw soldiers of the Eleventh Kansas scouted the Republican River valley to Fort Kearny, Nebraska. A shortage of horses, equipment, and other supplies continually hampered the command in attempting to protect the Santa Fe Trail between Council Grove and Fort Larned. Tensions along the Santa Fe Trail increased during the summer of 1864, prompting Major General Samuel R. Curtis, commander of the military district, to organize an expedition in July 1864. With four hundred men and two artillery pieces, he arrived at Walnut Creek crossing in early July and established Fort Zarah before proceeding on to Fort Larned. Curtis sent additional troops to strengthen the garrisons at Forts Larned and Ellsworth. But his columns never encountered any Indians while on the march. After the Eleventh Kansas returned to Fort Riley on August 8 the raids resumed.

On August 9 General Curtis ordered Major General Blunt to continue the offensive, organizing a force of six hundred men from Fort Riley and other posts. His orders were to harass Indians during the crucial autumn months when they would cease raiding and concentrate on laying in the winter's supply of buffalo meat. But Blunt's campaign proved no more successful than Curtis's effort. He claimed routing fifteen hundred to three thousand Indians in a battle northwest of Fort Larned on September 25. In actuality, the battle was little more than a skirmish, and Blunt pursued the Indians for two days until his horses gave out. He then returned to Fort Riley.

Indian attacks escalated rapidly after the brutal November massacre of peaceful Cheyennes at Sand Creek, Colorado Territory, by Colonel John M. Chivington of the Third Colorado Cavalry. Prior to Chivington's attack, Major Edward W. Wynkoop, commander at Fort Lyon, Colorado, had accepted the surrender of several hundred Arapahos and Cheyennes. But this did not sit well with Major B.S. Henning at Fort Riley, temporary commander of the District of the Upper Arkansas. He believed Wynkoop's peaceful actions violated General Curtis's announcement that "I want no peace till the Indians suffer more." Henning replaced Wynkoop with Major Scott Anthony of Chivington's regiment and ordered Wynkoop to Fort Riley to explain his actions. Anthony then cooperated with Colonel Chivington to set up the Sand Creek Massacre.

After this brutal attack, young Cheyenne Dog Soldiers and Arapahos attacked stagecoaches and wagon trains, burned ranches, seized cattle and horses, and killed dozens of people. Settlers from the Saline, Solomon, and Little Blue River valleys were driven eastward. Fort Riley

During the summer of 1864 Major General Samuel R. Curtis led a military expedition from Fort Riley to prevent Indians from closing the Santa Fe Trail. In July he established Fort Zarah and proceeded to Fort Larned. He sent additional soldiers to strengthen Forts Ellsworth and Larned, which suppressed hostilities. But once troops returned to Fort Riley, Indian raids resumed.

In 1864 General James Blunt was placed in command of the newly created District of the Upper Arkansas, headquartered at Fort Riley.

troops patrolled to the Smoky Hill crossing west of Salina while a detached column was placed on duty at Council Grove. Cavalry from Fort Riley once again escorted the mails and the stage lines, but raids continued. The following month Cheyennes and Arapahos struck isolated settlements along the valley of the Little Blue. Indians also stampeded horses belonging to a company of Seventh Iowa Cavalry troopers encamped near a stage crossing close to Salina. The same soldiers were attacked a week later resulting in the deaths of four troopers. Kiowas raided Fort Larned and stole 172 cavalry mounts. The frontier was in chaos, and settlers gathered in armed groups.

While the Indian situation on the Central Plains remained tense, a new threat appeared on the Kansas–Missouri border. Confederate general Sterling Price moved northward with twelve thousand men, hoping to restore Missouri to the Confederacy, but settling for plunder, new recruits for his army, and the destruction of Union military installations. As Price turned westward to Kansas in October 1864, General Curtis invoked martial law and asked Governor Thomas Carney to call out the entire state militia. Although poorly armed and trained, ten thousand militia joined the four thousand soldiers that Curtis had stripped from Fort Riley and elsewhere to form the Army of the Border.

Price's army drove General Blunt and part of the Kansas troops out of Lexington, Missouri. Blunt's men were delaying Price while General Curtis prepared defenses along the Big Blue River. At the Battle of Westport, Missouri, October 23, 1864, the combined forces of General Curtis and General Alfred Pleasonton defeated Price's army. Two days later Pleasonton's cavalry routed Price's men as they fought a rear-guard action at the Battle of Mine Creek in Linn County, Kansas. This action marked the end of organized Confederate operations in the Trans-Mississippi region although guerrilla activity persisted to the war's end. Following Price's defeat, General Curtis sent the militia home, and the veteran volunteer companies returned to Forts Riley and Leavenworth.

In December eight companies of the Second Colorado Cavalry arrived at Fort Riley. But their stay was temporary as these companies quickly left for Forts Ellsworth and Zarah. These additional troops had been called to Kansas for the coming spring offensive against the Plains Indians. Among these troops was the Second U.S. Volunteer Infantry, comprised of "Galvanized Yankees," that is, former Confederate prisoners of war who were pardoned by joining up to fight Indians. In March troops traveled to reinforce Fort Kearny, while Brevet Brigadier General James H. Ford took twelve hundred cavalry from Fort Riley to Indian encampments along the Cimarron River and Crooked Creek. By the time Ford's columns reached Fort Larned, Indian agents had begun peace talks. The troops returned to Fort Riley before once again dispersing. The peace talks with the Cheyennes, Arapahos, and Kiowas led to the treaties of Fort Sully and the Little Arkansas. In return for not molesting travelers on the overland trails, the tribes would receive increased annuities.

The garrison anxiously awaited editions of the *Soldier's Letter*, the Second Colorado Cavalry's newspaper published at Fort Riley. Throughout the early weeks of 1865 all the local newspapers relayed bits

At the end of the Civil War a number of regiments passed through Fort Riley to be mustered out of service, among them the Fifteenth Kansas Cavalry, of which members of Company F are depicted here.

of news from the Civil War: General William T. Sherman's successes in Georgia, rumors of a peace conference, and the capture of Richmond. The issue that might have announced the war's end instead was printed with black borders between the columns to mourn the death of President Lincoln. Word of the assassination arrived by stage in the early hours of April 17—four years to the day since word of the war's beginning had reached the fort.

But the fighting between the North and the South finally had come to an end. For most of the volunteer soldiers who passed through Fort Riley that summer and fall, their thoughts were of mustering out and returning home. Companies from the Second and Fifth U.S. Volunteers, Twelfth Kansas Infantry, Fifteenth Kansas Cavalry, and Ninth Wisconsin Artillery passed through Riley to be mustered out of service.

Thus ended the Civil War experiences at Fort Riley. Stretched thin between their many duties, the volunteer soldiers repeatedly demonstrated the value of Fort Riley as an outpost. Because of the troops' actions during the Civil War, in 1865 the army accepted the plan to use fixed central posts to launch offensive operations. Thus any fort with a central location and transportation connections would be vital to the effective implementation of this strategy. Expenses would again become an issue with a post-war cost-cutting Congress, thus complicating the army's missions. Fort Riley's future remained tied to protecting the frontier and maintaining peace. But that mission faced new realities as the boundary separating settlement and frontier continued to shrink.

6

The Frontier Army

The end of the Civil War redirected the nation's attention to settling the frontier. In the spring of 1866 veterans and foreign immigrants began pouring onto the Great Plains seeking land and opportunity. Aiding this westward thrust was the construction of the Union Pacific Railroad. One rail line followed the Kansas River valley—from Kansas City to Lawrence, Topeka, and beyond. Down this same route, a little more than a decade before, the first soldiers had marched to establish Fort Riley. In the brief years since its establishment, Fort Riley had served its purpose well. As settlement spread westward, Fort Riley's troops would continue their traditional pre-war mission of protecting the new towns and farms, the long established trails and stage routes to Santa Fe and along the Smoky Hill River to Denver, and construction workers building rail lines westward.

During the last months of 1865, as Civil War volunteer units mustered out, regular army troops returned to Fort Riley. Four companies of the Thirteenth U.S. Infantry arrived in September and assumed the duties and responsibilities from departing Kansas and Colorado volunteers. The Thirteenth soon was joined by two companies of the Second U.S. Cavalry. These units contained both recent recruits and hardened veterans who had witnessed tough campaigns in the western and eastern theaters.

The general condition of the post occupied the commanding officer's attention, as it had before the Civil War. Throughout the winter and spring months carpenters, painters, and plasterers repaired the barracks, quarters, and work buildings. In early March 1866 Major John W. Davidson, Second Cavalry, arrived from Fort Fletcher (later renamed Fort Hays) and assumed command of the post. That May, Davidson wrote a critical and strategic analysis of the present and future utilization of Fort Riley. His report anticipated the plan for this post during the remainder of the century:

> As a station of troops to protect settlements in event of Indian hostilities Fort Riley has lost its importance; settlements being well in advance of it on both the Smoky Hill and Republican Rivers. But as a Depot for the supply of the posts in our western Territories, and in view of this point being the supply point of the new Mexican trade (if the Union Pacific Railway runs up the Republican) it is of great importance to the Government.
>
> This should be, in my opinion, the Cavalry Depot of the West. The Government owns a large reserve here; the facilities for grazing are unsurpassable in the West; and by encouraging the growth of grain by purchase in open market in small lots, instead of the odious contract system it can be gotten cheaply and sufficiently in the vicinity. The remount horses of all the cavalry posts on the Platte, Smoky Hill and Arkansas should be kept here.
>
> The recruits for the companies should be sent here, and after a few months careful training, distributed. Again during the winter months, much of the cavalry west might be drawn in here and subsisted and recuperated for the renewals of active work.

New recruits would find the buildings in fair condition and the stables able to accommodate four hundred horses.

In April, Davidson and the Third U.S. Infantry escorted General John Pope on an inspection tour of the military department. Pope had recently arrived to assume command of the Department of the Missouri, headquartered at Fort Leavenworth. Pope's pre-Civil War background as a topographical engineer on the frontier helped him appreciate the value of the railroad and telegraph in the vast distances of the Plains. The army hoped to improve communication and transportation between the "settled" area near Fort Riley and the distant forts to its west. The arrival of the railroad at Riley in the fall of 1866 signaled the army's increasing ability to project supply bases and outposts farther west. The relationship between the army at Fort Riley and the nation's railroads was symbiotic from the start. The Union Pacific, Eastern Division, was established in 1866 because of Fort Riley's central location and the avail-

The coming of the railroad was possibly the most significant event in opening the West, and its network of transportation and communication placed Fort Riley at a strategic central location. But as the railroad facilitated settlement, Indians became increasing disturbed by this threat to their hunting lands.

ability of troops to protect construction crews. The railroad's capacity to move men, horses, and supplies would be vital to the survival of the fort.

The post garrison also continued its traditional escort duties. These details, usually numbering fewer than twenty men, provided protection for railroad work crews, smaller wagon trains, U.S. mail deliveries, agents delivering annuities to Indians, and most important to the soldiers, the army paymaster. Such duties could be boring or dangerous, but the enlisted men preferred these details to fatigue assignments on the post.

At the end of the Civil War the government authorized the creation of four new cavalry regiments needed to patrol the Plains. These units were the Seventh, Eighth, Ninth, and Tenth U.S. Cavalry regiments (the Ninth and Tenth being formed of black troops, also known as "buffalo soldiers"). In late August 1866 notification arrived that four hundred recruits for one of the new cavalry regiments would soon arrive. Designated originally as the "Eighth Cavalry" this regiment became the Seventh U.S. Cavalry on September 26, 1866. Organizing, outfitting, and deploying the regiment consumed the remainder of the year. Concern heightened that arriving recruits were bringing the dreaded cholera.

This is the earliest known photograph of Fort Riley, taken in the fall of 1866 or early 1867. The photographer is located in the same general area (northwest of the post) where Private Gaddis had sketched his image a few years before. This photo was included in a Quartermaster Department study being conducted at the post.

Post commander Captain Henry Noyes ordered a floor, doors, and windows fitted to the original territorial legislature stone building at Pawnee to transform the building into a hospital. There also was urgent need to secure bedsacks, overcoats, and blankets for the incoming soldiers.

The new cavalry recruits began arriving in early September and bivouacked at the former Pawnee townsite. By the end of the month 701 men were present, of which 66 were sick and 38 were under arrest or confinement. Over the next two months officers organized the men into twelve companies, issued uniforms and equipment, and drilled them in the rudiments of military tactics and training. The Seventh was far from being a crack regiment, and its officers had little plains or Indian fighting experience. Major Alfred Gibbs arrived in October to take temporary command of the regiment.

By November several companies of the Seventh Cavalry were sufficiently outfitted to be deployed at other posts. Fort Riley was the official headquarters of the Seventh Cavalry, but like other regiments before and after the Civil War, most of the troops left Fort Riley after training

The post hospital was one of the first buildings constructed at Fort Riley. This photograph was taken prior to the 1872 addition of a second floor.

to garrison other frontier forts. Other officers and recruits continued to arrive at Riley, including regimental commander Colonel Andrew J. Smith and Lieutenant Colonel George A. Custer. For all practical purposes, Custer was in command of the regiment owing to Smith's detached service duties. This became official in February 1867 when Smith was named commander of the District of the Upper Arkansas. Custer gathered around him intensely loyal lieutenants who contributed to the factionalism that infested the regiment. Feuding between groups of officers was common; West Point officers feuded with civilian appointees as did old army regulars with new recruits.

Custer quickly became alarmed by the large number of desertions. This situation highlighted a new reality confronting the post-war army. Frontier regiments were not filled with men imbued with a sense of cause and mission. These recruits did not fully understand or appreciate the notion of military service and obligation. Many others were offended by the martinet behavior or harsh discipline of their commanding officer, or they left for better paying jobs. A private earned sixteen dollars per month in 1867, while Fort Riley's post quartermaster was hiring civilian teamsters for at least thirty dollars a month. Consequently, Custer's command was riddled with desertions. By the end of 1866, 80 out of 963 recruits had deserted.

Fort Riley was the official headquarters for the Seventh U.S. Cavalry, although most troops left after training to garrison other frontier posts. This 1867 sketch from Harper's Weekly depicts a battle between Cheyennes and Company G of the Seventh near Fort Wallace.

During this time General William T. Sherman, commander of the Division of the Missouri, arrived at Fort Riley to survey the "Indian problem" on the frontier. His notions of dealing with Native Americans were shaped by his Civil War experience. Specifically, Sherman believed in a total war against Indians who might stand in the way of advancing civilization. This strategy required strong columns of cavalry and infantry that could seek out and defeat their targets.

The resumption of travel across Kansas to the Colorado goldfields and the construction of the railroad angered the Indians, who once again saw their lands invaded, grasses and timber destroyed, and their buffalo killed. Traffic increased in September 1865 when the Butterfield Overland Despatch began running three stages a week between Atchison and Denver, all going through Fort Riley. Travel also heightened as wagons loaded with hay and other supplies departed from Fort Riley to posts farther west. The Little Arkansas treaties in October 1865 supposedly promised safe transit along the trails, stipulating that Cheyennes, Arapahos, Kiowas, and Comanches reside south of Kansas and away from "the overland routes already established." The treaties allowed the tribes to hunt as far north in Kansas as the Arkansas River. However, some Indians continued to return farther north to their traditional hunting lands, which the new stage routes crossed.

Concerned that hostilities were imminent, General Pope ordered that no wagon trains with fewer than twenty-five wagons and thirty fighting men could head west. Fort Riley served as the staging ground for these journeys.

Signs of future troubles were obvious. Cheyennes stampeded the horse herd at Fort Wallace, attacks on stage stations increased, and by April 1867 only one station in four was still operating along the Smoky Hill route. Most dramatically, in December 1866 the Sioux killed the impetuous Captain William Fetterman and his entire command of eighty men near Fort Phil Kearny, in present Wyoming. This event shocked and outraged the army. Generals Sherman and Sheridan feared that if the army did not forcefully respond to this defeat the Arapahos, Kiowas, and Comanches would be encouraged to attack travelers and outposts when the spring grass sprouted. Once the grasses formed their horses could feed better, thus increasing the Plains tribes' mobility and aggression. When Cheyenne attacks intensified in the spring, driving most of the settlers from the Solomon River valley, military commanders authorized a show of force to punish "treaty violators" and prevent further expansion of hostilities.

Troops of the Seventh Cavalry moved to Fort Larned to prepare for the expedition. A snow storm and a week of freezing temperatures

Lieutenant Colonel George Armstrong Custer and his wife arrived at Fort Riley in November 1866 as the Seventh U.S. Cavalry organized in the vicinity of the territorial capital at Pawnee. In the absence of the regimental colonel, Andrew Smith, Custer not only commanded the regiment but also was the ranking officer on post. His tenure as the fort's commanding officer was marked by high desertion and other administrative problems as he attempted to organize the newly created regiment from post-Civil War recruits. In the spring of 1867 Custer departed the post with his regiment to pursue Indians in what came to be known as Hancock's expedition. The ill-fated campaign accomplished little, and Custer found himself court-martialed for returning to Fort Riley without clear authority to do so.

delayed the main body of fourteen hundred men at Fort Riley. Finally on March 27 General Winfield Scott Hancock led four companies of the Seventh Cavalry, Battery B of the Fourth U.S. Artillery, and seven companies of the Thirty-seventh Infantry out of Fort Riley for an expedition down the Santa Fe Trail. According to Major Albert Barnitz of the Seventh Cavalry, inclement weather and whiskey dealers plagued the column all the way to Fort Larned. Army Surgeon Isaac Coates complained that the cold weather and Kansas thaws "wore out the men and told severely on the cavalry horses and mule teams." At Fort Larned Hancock confronted a delegation of Indian chiefs who were still angered by Chivington's treachery at Sand Creek. Dismissing the chiefs' warnings, Hancock marched his command toward Pawnee Fork, the location of a large Oglala Sioux and Cheyenne Dog Soldier encampment. Before Hancock's columns reached the village hundreds of warriors prepared for battle blocked his path. A major battle was avoided only through the intervention of Indian Agent Edward Wynkoop. Fearing a repeat of the Sand Creek Massacre, the occupants of the encampment fled during the night. This convinced Hancock that the Indians were neither peaceful nor trustworthy, and he ordered Custer and the Seventh Cavalry to pursue them. The Cheyennes scattered into smaller parties, eluding and totally frustrating their pursuers. Custer found the Smoky Hill Road in panic with stage stations burned and settlers killed. When a courier reported these depredations to Hancock, he ordered the Pawnee Fork village burned. This act only intensified Indian raids throughout the summer on railroad surveyors and work crews and on stage stations and wagon trains along the Arkansas, Smoky Hill, and Platte Rivers.

Custer and his cavalry were ordered to remain in the field and punish the guilty Indians. But weeks of pursuit resulted in few sightings, only some inconclusive skirmishes, and the total exhaustion of men and horses. For the remainder of the summer Hancock's forces remained on the defensive. To assist patrolling the overland travel routes, Kansas governor Samuel Crawford organized the Eighteenth Kansas Volunteer Cavalry into service.

While Custer and his troops conducted operations against the Indians, 116 men of Company K, Thirty-eighth Infantry, reached Fort Riley on June 11. They were en route to Fort Harker but floodwaters washed out railroad bridges and trestles, suspending traffic for some time. The arrival of this unit is significant because it was blamed for bringing cholera to Fort Riley. As the summer progressed, the several forts in Kansas reported the appearance of the dreaded disease.

General Winfield Scott Hancock left Fort Riley in March 1867 with troops of the Seventh Cavalry, Fourth Artillery, and Thirty-seventh Infantry to begin a campaign along the Santa Fe Trail. Having little understanding of Indians, Hancock was ineffective in his efforts, and his expedition resulted in increased warfare in the region. (Below) Hancock's burning of an Indian village on Pawnee Fork, April 19, 1867. The sketch by Theodore Davis is from Harper's Weekly, *June 8, 1867.*

The first case of cholera at Fort Riley occurred June 22 when a quartermaster employee became ill and died later that same day. Two days later Post Surgeon Bernard John Dowling Irwin ordered all latrines and wash areas cleansed, whitewashed, and provided with ventilators. He further ordered enlisted quarters and those of civil employees to be kept "scrupulously cleaned" and "all garbage and other offensive matter to be removed to a safe distance." Kitchens received new slop barrels, and everyone was made strictly accountable for the sanitary conditions of the post. Irwin recommended a general clean-up of the post every Saturday. Eventually cholera afflicted fifty-nine persons, and twenty-nine died at Fort Riley during the summer of 1867.

Throughout July and August, Custer continued leading several companies of his regiment across the plains of western Kansas and eastern Colorado in an attempt to locate his elusive Indian foes. Bad weather (in this case extreme heat) and incompetent guides continued plaguing the Fort Riley columns. The futile campaign only exhausted his men and horses, which now needed time for rest and resupply. Lured by the proximity of the Colorado goldfields and worn down by the conditions of the chase, ninety men deserted in just six weeks. Custer left his command at Fort Wallace to seek new orders at Forts Harker or Riley. He led a small detachment on a forced march of 150 miles in some fifty-five hours. This caused more desertions and the deaths of two troopers Custer sent back alone to find his spare mare.

At Fort Harker Custer secured leave in the middle of the night from a sleepy Colonel Smith and boarded the morning train for Fort Riley and a reunion with his wife. The next morning when Colonel Smith heard the full story of Custer's march he ordered him arrested and preferred charges against him for being absent from his command without leave and conduct to the prejudice of good order and military discipline. This charge stemmed from complaints that Custer drove his men and horses to exhaustion and did not attend to their needs, thus causing desertions and leaving the remainder unfit for action. Later that fall a court-martial at Fort Leavenworth suspended Custer from rank and command for one year along with forfeiture of pay. The Seventh Cavalry would not return to Fort Riley for two decades, long after Custer's 1876 debacle at the Little Bighorn.

In early August 1867 the Tenth Cavalry's regimental headquarters under the command of Colonel Benjamin Grierson arrived at Riley from Fort Leavenworth. Grierson had risen through the ranks during the Civil War and now commanded one of two black mounted units organized following the war. Accompanying Grierson were 122 recruits who found the post in "very bad order." Despite Surgeon Irwin's sanitary directives, grounds around the officers' and enlisted men's quarters remained covered with a heavy growth of weeds, and barracks were not supplied with bunks. Grierson put his command to work cleaning up and repairing the post. Troops I, K, L, and M organized and outfitted at Fort Riley for service on the frontier. The regimental headquarters remained at Riley until the following spring.

Since Hancock's campaign failed to defeat the Indians, energies turned toward a new peace treaty. Congress created a peace commission that met with southern tribesmen at Medicine Lodge in October 1867.

The treaty signed there defined two large reservations in Indian Territory (present Oklahoma)—one for Cheyennes and Arapahos and the other for Kiowas, Comanches, and Kiowa–Apaches. The federal government would provide these tribes with clothing and other annuities while they learned to support themselves through agriculture. But because Cheyenne Dog Soldiers insisted that the treaty guarantee their right to hunt along the Republican and Smoky Hill Rivers in Kansas, the potential for trouble between Indians and advancing white settlers continued.

An uneasy and temporary peace descended on the Kansas frontier. But the transfer of troops continued, and Fort Riley served as a collection point for these movements. In mid-November the *Junction City Weekly Union* reported, "Military movements have been quite brisk the past week, looking much like old times, before a railroad carried everything swiftly by us." Between November and December the troop population at Fort Riley increased from 233 soldiers to 558 as six companies of the Tenth Cavalry went into winter quarters. These companies remained until the spring of 1868 when they moved to their new frontier stations. Replacing them were companies of the Third and Fifth Infantry regiments.

The next two years witnessed a predictable pattern: spring and summer alarm over Indian movements with occasional attacks upon settlements. This brought forth a quick military response. While most of this

Indian attacks were frequent throughout 1867 and continued during the next two years. While most action was removed from the Fort Riley area, troops were called out in response to hostilities and to protect settlements. This sketch is of an 1868 attack near Sheridan, Kansas.

action was far removed from Fort Riley, occasional flare-ups required sending troops from the post. In August 1868 Fort Riley received reports of "outrages" committed by approximately forty Indians on the Solomon Fork of the Smoky Hill. Captain Simon Snyder and one company of infantry left Fort Riley on August 15 to afford "protection to the settlements." The following May messengers brought news that Indians had killed six settlers in Jewell County. As a result, an expedition of seven officers and 184 mounted men left the fort to "punish hostile Indians." Such quick responses offered temporary reassurance to the citizens living in the area, but the troops usually failed to apprehend the offenders and only managed to exhaust men and horses. On this latter expedition, Captain William Graham, in a June 19 letter to his wife, expressed his frustration at the cavalry's inability to locate the elusive foe:

> Here we are again at the same place I wrote you from a week ago last night. We left our camp on the Republican the night of the 17th a report having come to me from Maj. Sinclair that one of his scouting parties has found a camp and trail of about 30 Indians near the mouth of Beaver Creek going south. I started immediately with a detachment consisting of Lieut. Merrimace & Hubbell and 40 men and marched all night; halting from 2-5am and then continuing on yesterday and following a large trail to Straight Creek making a distance marched of about 46 miles, but we lost the trail there, and have been unable all day

today to find it again; so we came here to camp on our way back and tomorrow will return to our camp on the Republican. We have had excellent weather since we have been out though very hot, but tonight it looks very much like as though it would rain hard, and if it does, we shall get a good soaking with nothing but our ponchos, overcoats, and saddle blankets to sleep on and under.

Fort Riley's involvement with protecting the frontier from Indian attack was decreasing as settlement continued west; the frontier was becoming a circumstance of the past. With Indians removed to reservations, the threat of attack was fast receding, and newer posts in the state such as Forts Hays and Larned were closer to any potential areas of conflict. By 1871 Fort Larned had replaced Fort Riley as the wagon train staging area, and the army had moved the quartermaster depot from Riley to Fort Harker. Harker, rather than Riley, became primarily responsible for shipments to interior forts. In the fall of 1878 Fort Riley troops were deployed to pursue a band of Cheyenne Dog Soldiers who had raided isolated communities in western Kansas. The raid and the pursuit are noteworthy as they marked the final armed clash between Indians and the army within Kansas.

7

A Time of Transition

The problem of balancing mission, manpower, and money was a continuing issue in Congress and thereby a continual problem for Fort Riley. With the Civil War over, Congress sought economy by slashing both the size and expenses of the army. The army no longer was the wartime protector of the nation, rather it was viewed with suspicions that dated back to the American Revolution, when the average citizen believed a large standing army in peacetime threatened his rights. Presidential use of the army to suppress legitimate labor strikes intensified this fear. Military spending opponents pointed to the "failure" of the 1865 Plains offensive, where six thousand troops killed fewer than one hundred Indians, yet the combined campaigns cost more than twenty million dollars. The vanishing frontier and the gradual shift of major campaigns northward during the 1870s brought Fort Riley's existence into question. The next thirty-five years of the fort's history were dominated by conflict: carrying out its mission in a changing West while surviving congressional calls for greater economy in the military budget.

In 1870 economy-minded congressmen cut a private's pay from sixteen dollars to thirteen dollars. This caused a staggering increase in desertions. During 1871 Fort Riley averaged twelve soldiers deserting each month, with forty-six doing so in November alone. Desertions amounted to more than 10 percent of the garrison.

In May 1869 companies from four different artillery regiments had arrived at Fort Riley to begin receiving instruction in light artillery

General John Schofield, commander of the Department of the Missouri, developed the idea to train regiments together in order to develop professional armies. As a result, in 1869 artillery regiments arrived at Fort Riley as part of an experimental artillery school of instruction. The program was discontinued in 1871, but a similar school would develop in later years and play a major role in Fort Riley's future.

tactics. This idea was the brainchild of General John Schofield, new commander of the Department of the Missouri, who as a professional soldier believed that the light batteries of the regular army needed to train together. Schofield believed the U.S. Army must be prepared to fight like the professional armies of Europe. That meant training the horse-drawn artillery from dispersed units to assemble quickly on the battlefield to provide massed firepower. Because of Fort Riley's size, location on a main rail line, and its stone barracks and stables, Schofield believed the post offered an ideal location to train artillery batteries. To implement his ideas four batteries of field artillery arrived at the post later that summer. Major John Hamilton of the First Artillery commanded the post during this experimental school's brief existence. But cost-cutting measures, combined with General Schofield's departure from the Department of the Missouri, ended the experimental artillery school of instruction. In March 1871 the terminated program and the batteries left Fort Riley for other posts.

In late April 1871 Captain Adna R. Chaffee brought a company of the Sixth U.S. Cavalry from Fort Richardson, Texas, to Fort Riley. That fall five other companies of the regiment joined these troops. Chaffee was another Civil War soldier who had risen through the ranks and earned his commission. During his tour of duty at Fort Riley, Chaffee married Annie Frances Rockwell, daughter of a prosperous Junction City businessman.

Between 1869 and 1871 the garrison frequently dwindled to less than half its designated normal strength. Influential citizens and neighboring communities, coveting the large military reservation, began questioning the need and proper use for Fort Riley. Forts Hays and Larned were assigned duties once held by Riley, and moving the quartermaster depot to Fort Harker meant the loss of government jobs and contracts for the communities surrounding Fort Riley, increasing their anxiety about the fort's future. Annual budgets for upkeep and repair of the post buildings shrank. Civilian and military pessimists believed that Fort Riley would soon be abandoned, but its central location and the size of its reservation would continue to be important, no matter how much the garrison size fluctuated.

Civilian attitudes toward the military largely reflected the opinion of the times: a standing army was only needed in times of crisis and was otherwise a burden to the taxpayer. Because the threat of Indian attack was diminishing some believed the fort no longer would be needed. The editor of the *Junction City Weekly Union* expressed this attitude as early as 1867: "the onward progress of the railroad, westward, will render useless to government the keeping up of such a military establishment as Fort Riley. It must before long be abandoned." The military held a different view as to the fort's usefulness as evidenced in early 1872 when a group of local citizens attempted to acquire part of the reservation for a private venture. These individuals received backing from Kansas governor James M. Harvey to annex seventy-one hundred acres of the reservation. The post commander, Lieutenant Colonel Thomas Neill, objected to the entire proposal, partly on the basis that General Sherman had stated, "every acre of land on this reservation was needed for military purposes."

While some elements of the civilian community thought only of themselves and hoped to reap personal economic advantage from the fort, one correspondent who visited the post expressed sympathy for the soldiers and their needs. He reflected on the realities of army life:

> Some people seeing these young gentlemen, fall to grumbling about the expense of the regular army, and all that sort of thing; but for our part we could not help remembering that same young gentleman, so careful now about fatigue uniforms and gloves and boots, and canes, might in a few months at the farthest be ordered off to some howling wilderness,

These artillery soldiers, posing in front of their barracks, are preparing for a dress parade. They are wearing the pattern 1888 dress uniform that included plumed helmet. A musician (with piped facings on his uniform) is standing second from the left.

to suffer all sorts of privations, and die, perhaps, by the handing of some skulking savage. It does not seem right, somehow, to quarrel with the gloves and boots of young gentlemen who, when the time comes, will ride at the word into the jaws of death.

As the spring of 1873 approached, the annual movement of troops from winter quarters in Fort Riley to the field was imminent. On April 20 five companies of the Sixth Cavalry left to establish summer headquarters near Fort Hays; they were positioned to protect travel routes and enforce the provisions of the Medicine Lodge treaties. Over the next six months the average garrison population was only thirty-seven soldiers.

In early September 1873 a fire destroyed four of the large stables. While all of the horses and mules were safely removed, the post suffered major losses of hay, harness, and equipment. The loss of these stables precluded maintaining more than one company of cavalry, and with budget cuts it was difficult to determine when they might be rebuilt. The following summer the stables remained in ashes, causing concern among Junction City businessmen. The weekly *Junction City Union* argued that if the fort was "put in shape" the cost of supplying the

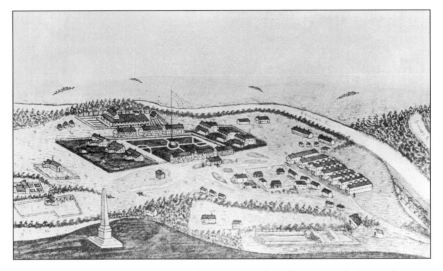

This ca. 1878 sketch by L. Ledue of the Sixteenth Infantry Band shows the general features of Fort Riley during the years the Sixteenth Infantry was stationed at the post. The fort is organized around a central parade ground with officers' quarters on the north and south sides and barracks on the east and west. East of the barracks is the post hospital. To the west are the guardhouse, magazine and quartermaster buildings, and stables. The post chapel and the chaplain's and post surgeon's quarters are on the north side. The Ogden Monument obelisk is in the foreground.

cavalry would be cheaper at Fort Riley than at Fort Hays. But bureaucracy and budget restraints caused the process to move slowly, and it was not until the end of the year that a Leavenworth contractor arrived to estimate repair costs.

The renewed support for Fort Riley expressed by the local press and the fort's civilian neighbors mirrored the changed economic conditions in the middle 1870s. The optimism and booming economy following the Civil War had been replaced by years of economic depression, grasshoppers, and drought. Increasingly over the next decade public opinion, as expressed in the local press, viewed the fort and federal money as vital to the local economy.

Repair of the stables proceeded slowly. A visit by the departmental inspector general gave impetus to further improvements to the fort. Unidentified officers suggested that abandoning Fort Leavenworth and making Fort Riley the general supply post for the southwest would create savings for the army. Such reports and opinions underscored

The Sixteenth U.S. Infantry garrisoned Fort Riley between 1877 and 1880 under the command of Colonel Galusha Pennypacker. In this ca. 1879 photo, members of the Sixteenth appear with the regiment's band.

the fact that the army had no intention of abandoning or closing Fort Riley.

The arrival of regimental headquarters staff and three companies of the Sixteenth Infantry in June 1877 ended nearly three years of garrisoning the post with skeletal companies. Colonel Galusha Pennypacker, commander of the Sixteenth, was the youngest general officer ever appointed in the United States service and also the youngest colonel ever to command a regiment of the regular army. Over the next year at least two companies of the Sixteenth regularly garrisoned Fort Riley while other troops left the fort on regular field duty and rapid response efforts. The garrison also performed ceremonial duties. In September 1879 a company marched to Neosho Falls in southeastern Kansas to participate in ceremonies welcoming President Rutherford B. Hayes and General William Sherman to the state.

Kansas weather posed a greater threat than Indians did to Fort Riley after the Civil War. In April 1880 buildings on the post suffered severe damage from a windstorm that swept through the area. Roofs were blown off, guttering torn away, and fences demolished. Even the flagpole in the center of the parade field was destroyed. The telegraph station in Junction City transmitted news of this disaster to the outside world. Fort Riley could not send word quickly because the telegraph line to the fort was not connected to an operating and staffed terminal. Outside communication was limited to army couriers and government ambulances. The latter delivered and retrieved messages in Junction City, including the mail, twice a day. It would be another three years (1883) before the fort would have telephone service. Updating communication facilities would be vital to Fort Riley's survival.

The three-year service of the Sixteenth Infantry at Fort Riley ended in early December 1880 as it was ordered to San Antonio, Texas. Replacing it were four companies of the Fourth Cavalry that had been stationed at Fort Garland, Colorado. Shortly after their arrival, the officers held a party in the garrison library hall with music provided by the regimental band and a "magnificent" supper served afterward. Prominent citizens from the area attended, including Governor John P. St. John and Mayor R.O. Rizer of Junction City. The following month Junction City community leaders reciprocated with a reception at the Bartell House.

Major Eugene Beaumont, the new post commander was not pleased with the physical condition of Fort Riley. He was especially angered by the condition of the post stables. Shortly after the Fourth Cavalry's arrival he wrote that a competent builder should inspect and rebuild the stables. Beaumont concluded, "As this post is one of the best in this Dept. on account of the fair condition of its buildings, its storage capacity, and the abundance and cleanliness of forage, it is reasonable to suppose that it will be the last to be abandoned, if at all. In view of this fact I would strongly urge that the stables may be rebuilt." In February 1881 twenty recruits passed through Fort Riley en route to Fort Hays, as the post continued its function as a routing stop for other forts. The appearance of new soldiers concerned a hardened veteran like Beaumont. To maintain the training and readiness of his soldiers he ordered daily company mounted drills. He also planned regular target practice later in the spring. Complicating this plan was the different weaponry in each company: some were equipped with Springfield rifles, some with Springfield carbines, and other with newer Hotchkiss carbines. All of these required different types of ammunition. As a cost-cutting measure the cavalry was not allotted extra ammunition for newer rifles, Gatling guns, and cannons. The men could only practice if the commanding officer was willing to personally pay for the ammunition. Such problems affected the professional efficiency of the service.

Major Beaumont also was concerned about the quality of the soldiers sent from recruiting depots. He complained to the adjutant general that "the reputation of the Army and lives and honor of its officers are continually impaired by inexperienced recruits, who are neither horsemen or marksmen." Beaumont demanded that the army recruit fully to its authorized size and form these additional men into companies as quickly as possible. Looking to the near future, he wanted replacements "in case of dangerous service during the coming summer and we must have men who have been identified for a few weeks with the regiment, or the greatest misfortune may await the command." Beaumont also wisely concluded that cavalry horses should become accustomed to firing before the troops rode them into combat. In response to this correspondence, the Fourth Cavalry received twenty recruits from depot on May 2. But despite Beaumont's wishes, the new recruits did not have long enough to train with other members of the Fourth Cavalry. One week later, four companies departed Fort Riley for Colorado to assist in maintaining order on the Unitah Reservation.

In November 1881 companies of the Ninth Cavalry under the command of Colonel Edward Hatch arrived, replacing the departing Fourth Cavalry. Like other Fort Riley commanders of the period, Hatch had served in the Civil War. The Ninth had spent the last fifteen years in Texas and New Mexico, and after garrisoning some of the most desolate outposts and fighting Kiowas and Comanches, the regiment moved to New Mexico for rest. Instead of relief they chased and fought Apaches and Utes across the deserts of the Southwest for another six years. The transfer of the Ninth to Fort Riley was viewed as a chance for troops to rest and reflect on their admirable combat record. Shortly after their arrival at Fort Riley, Lieutenant Colonel Nathan A.M. Dudley wrote of the Ninth Cavalry soldier:

> I consider that the discipline of the troops at Ft. Riley will compare favorably with that of any troops in the Army. Dress parade is held every evening except Saturday's. One drill each day has been held the last month when the weather permitted. Target practice has been commenced. . . . Guard Mount is most carefully & accurately held, and while the troops only have the undress blouse, and fatigue cap to appear in, a cleaner guard I have never seen mounted in the Department. . . . At present the command is in need of boots.

Military bands were important in providing not only musical aires for parades and retreat ceremonies, but their musical talents also were put to use on social occasions. A case in point occurred at Fort Riley around December 1880, shortly after the arrival of the Fourth Cavalry: a party was held "with music provided by the regimental band." The musicians shown here at Fort Riley compose the Sixteenth Infantry Band.

But not even the Ninth Cavalry could defend Fort Riley against Kansas weather. The fort was hit by a tornado in April 1882, which unroofed and partially destroyed one set of quarters and heavily damaged outbuildings of four other sets of quarters and barracks. The commissary and quartermaster buildings also were unroofed, and three soldiers were seriously injured. The post quartermaster estimated damages to be thirty thousand dollars, but the Quartermaster Department could only allocate four thousand dollars for repairs. Fort Riley also needed other upgrades. These included chimneys in the barracks, which had never drawn well and had become carbonated over nearly three decades of use, creating a serious health hazard. The stables needed attention, this because of shoddy workmanship when rebuilt several years before. Writers in the *Army and Navy Journal* speculated that Fort Riley might have to be abandoned.

Hatch returned from detached service in Indian Territory two weeks after the tornado and wrote a letter to the departmental inspector general addressing a recurring issue of the frontier army: troop readiness versus their use in pulling fatigue duty on post. He wrote that it was evident the soldiers required drill and schools of instruction to bring them up to a proper standard. But to accomplish this, Hatch argued, it was necessary to relieve the soldiers from duty as laborers and teamsters. He concluded, "It would be infinitely preferable for the . . . companies to take the field in Colorado than [be] occupied in rebuilding Ft. Riley."

The Ninth took pride that the first black chaplain appointed in the army was assigned to their unit in the fall of 1884. Chaplain Henry V. Plummer, an ex-slave from Maryland and a graduate of Howard University, brought a sense of dedication and enthusiasm to his work. A writer for the *Army and Navy Journal* would declare, "The morals of this command will bear comparison with the most moral post of the Army, if you will name it. There is far less drunkenness and crime than in any town of its size in moral Kansas."

Dedicated to keeping his troops prepared for field service, Hatch instituted drill twice weekly and held schools for officers in the evening. Company commanders also were required to hold classes for noncommissioned officers three nights a week. This was not tactical training but basic education to improve the literacy of the regiment. In mid-June 1884 two companies of the Ninth Cavalry left for assignment in Fort Lewis, Colorado. They returned to Fort Riley in October, going into winter quarters and resuming their usual garrison duties.

The following summer and fall of 1885 companies of the Ninth again were ordered to the field. This time they took up station in Indian Territory to keep land speculators and "boomers" out of these lands. The following summer the buffalo soldiers of the Ninth Cavalry were replaced by the Fifth Cavalry.

8

Permanent Military Post

The decade of the 1880s loomed as one of challenge for the army in defining its future. Decisions made during this time addressed the army's renewed concerns for professionalism and troop training that Generals Sherman and Schofield raised after the Civil War. As army leaders looked to that future, they questioned what to do with the nearly two hundred forts built nationally during the nineteenth century. Congress and the army began moving toward creating the "permanent posts" advocated by General Sherman. His plan required consolidating limited resources and manpower to missions better suited to the reality confronting a post-frontier army. For Kansas it meant closing seven of its nine forts by 1890, leaving only Forts Riley and Leavenworth.

All the army's priorities made Fort Riley a perfect match. Its location and connection with railroad networks was very important. Railroad promoters in Junction City had made sure that the fort was connected to the Union Pacific at Kearney, Nebraska, and with both the Missouri, Kansas and Texas railroad and the Atchison, Topeka and Santa Fe at Emporia. Combined with the post's original connection to the Union Pacific, Eastern Division, Fort Riley was at the center of the nation's railroad network. This was more than coincidence. Steam locomotives needed water, and their tracks followed the old wagon trails, trails that led again to Fort Riley. This central location and railroad web meant inexpensive transportation and supply costs to the post. Troops could be wintered on the large post and then shipped out for summer campaigning.

Fort Riley's large acreage was of vital importance to the post's role as a supply depot. By 1880 the fort had developed a hay farm, shipping this product by rail to cavalry posts across the United States. This photo of hay ready to load and ship was taken in the early twentieth century.

The large original reservation also was important as a supply depot. Fort Riley became a hay farm, with the army shipping this product by rail to cavalry posts in arid regions of the nation. Starting in 1880 three hundred tons of hay were shipped to Fort Garland, Colorado, for winter supplies. Forts Wingate and Craig, both in New Mexico, also received hay, shipped from Fort Riley less expensively than they could receive it from local suppliers. These reduced expenses could not be ignored by military planners or congressional cost-cutters.

Fort Riley being an ideal location for a cavalry training school tied closely to a plan long advocated by William T. Sherman, who believed in developing a system of post schools, each specializing in training specific military branch skills. In 1882 he ordered a survey on the feasibility of maintaining permanent military posts, a directive that would have long-ranging affects on Fort Riley.

Dating back to the close of the Civil War, some military planners believed that the size and geography of the Fort Riley military reservation was ideal for training cavalry. Now, echoing the sentiments of Major John W. Davidson nearly two decades before, higher command formulated plans ensuring Fort Riley's existence into the twentieth century. This was part of a growing movement toward professionalism long advocated by innovative leaders such as William Sherman, commanding general of the army from 1869 to 1883. During his tenure he advocated creation of a system of post schools, each specializing in training specific military branch skills. Congressional critics had long contended that the expensive cavalry was just lightly armed mounted infantry, and cavalry officers admitted their units were never trained to fight while mounted. The Infantry and Cavalry School at Fort Leavenworth, established in 1881, was an early response to such criticism.

Sherman addressed the need to consolidate military posts and establish permanent garrisons in his 1881 report to the secretary of war. He stated, "The time for temporary shanties has passed away, and no building should henceforth be erected at any of the permanent forts and military establishments except of stone or brick." The following year, he ordered a survey on the feasibility of maintaining permanent posts.

Major General John M. Schofield, once again in command of the Division of the Missouri (which included Fort Riley), elaborated on Sherman's arguments by explaining the issue of adequate living quarters as they affected the daily lives of soldiers under his command:

> The necessity is very urgent for liberal appropriations to provide permanent shelter for troops in this division. The period of "temporary huts" for the troops is passed. The tide of civilization has crossed the continent, the Indians have been located upon reservations, near which considerable bodies of troops must be stationed to preserve order and prevent or suppress any outbreak. Concentration of the troops at these, and a few other points of great strategic importance, is now possible, and should, on all accounts, be affected without delay. The stations to be occupied are no longer temporary in their nature, but permanent posts, and they should be provided with comfortable barracks and quarters. It is neither just nor wise to continue the occupation of the temporary huts which were hastily and cheaply constructed, and which are now in a state of decay, some of them located where the troops can perform no possible good service, but where they must be kept because they cannot be quartered elsewhere.

General Schofield raised the issue of proper training for the army's artillery. Newer breech-loading weapons required greater open range for practice, and modern military tactics required massed artillery for greater effectiveness. Only Fort Riley, argued Schofield, provided the sufficient firing range away from congested urban areas. In addition, it had space to house the artillerymen while practicing together.

In November 1883 Sherman retired, and his longtime colleague and friend Philip H. Sheridan assumed command of the army. Sheridan came to the post after a long and distinguished career beginning before the Civil War. A cavalryman by instinct and training, he had for many years commanded the Division of the Missouri. His post-Civil War duties involved pacification of the Trans-Mississippi West, which made him familiar with the advantages and disadvantages of distant, isolated posts. Sheridan understood that consolidating army posts and increasing professionalism were signposts to the future. He realized the need to improve cavalry training and believed Fort Riley afforded the perfect location do so. In his first report to Congress in 1884 he stated:

> I feel deeply interested in improvement of the cavalry arm of the service. . . . By a wise interposition, the Government has retained. . . . Fort Riley, Kansas, a beautiful, large reservation. The post and its

*Upon the retirement of General Sherman, Philip Sher-
idan assumed command of the army and was instrumental in obtaining authorization and funding for the
Cavalry and Light Artillery School at Fort Riley. He
looked upon the post as an important piece of real
estate to be retained by the army. Sheridan's persis-
tence in establishing the school secured the future of
the fort and transformed it into one of the army's most
important educational and training centers.*

reservation are situated on the Kansas River, in the garden spot of
Kansas. . . . It is now contemplated to make it a headquarters for the
cavalry of the Army.

Reflecting the economic realities of maintaining the army's most expensive arm, Sheridan pointed out:

At that place many of the cavalry horses which every year become
broken down or otherwise temporarily unfit for service could

recuperate and be reissued to troops in a condition fifty percent better than that of the new, untrained horses we annually buy from farmers. If the commercial value of horses continues to increase as rapidly as during the past ten years, it may become necessary to raise the horses needed for our military service, and Fort Riley is a place where the Government might advantageously breed such horses for its own use, as is done in continental Europe.

Since its establishment, Fort Riley, like other frontier forts, had suffered neglect in maintaining its buildings. Current structures had been patched and repaired so often over the years that their structural integrity was questionable. Evidence of this appeared in an inspector general's March 1884 report, which described the repairs needed to buildings on the post:

> Barracks No. 2, 4, and 5 need new ceilings & porches. Officers Quarters No. 1 and 2 needs repairs of roof; No. 8 & 12 need repairs on porches. Stables 1, 2, 3, & 5: The mangers and feed boxes are in a very dilapidated condition and as they cannot be repaired ought to be rebuilt. IN their present condition they are dangerous and liable at any time to seriously injure if not kill some of the horses. Privies—the privies now in use by Troops H, L, M Ninth Cavalry at this post are in a very dilapidated conditions. They cannot be repaired and for the health of the command they should at once be replaced by new ones.
>
> No addition alterations were made last year to either Barracks or Quarters.
>
> But there are not sufficient quarters for the officers.

Such conditions soon received the personal attention of General Sheridan. In late spring and early summer of 1885 he and General Nelson Miles visited the post to assess what new buildings and other improvements were needed at Fort Riley to establish a school. The weekly *Junction City Union* reported the inspection found the post to be in "very bad shape" but that work would soon commence to make Riley a full regimental post and the principal cavalry depot of the army.

In September 1885 Captain George Pond arrived at Fort Riley to oversee construction. He was the first officer from the Quartermaster Department assigned to Fort Riley since the depot was removed in 1867. Pond, a native of Connecticut, had served in the Civil War with an infantry unit from that state. But continuing problems from wounds received in the Civil War led him to seek transfer to the Quartermaster Department in the fall of 1883.

Captain George Pond arrived at Fort Riley in 1885 and was placed in charge of construction efforts. During the next six years Pond oversaw many facets of the fort's "modernization" to make it the army's cavalry training center. As a result, more than thirty new buildings were constructed, and a modern water works and electrical system further helped transform the frontier fort into an important center for army education. Pond served in the Civil War as an enlisted man and later graduated from the U.S. Military Academy. His cavalry service and military management skills were important elements in establishing the infrastructure support for the Cavalry and Light Artillery School, which began operation in 1892.

Constructing the new barracks began while several older buildings were being repaired. Most of the work involved sections of the original post and therefore did not require detailed planning. By May 1886 these structures were renovated and occupied. Consideration of "re-designing" the post awaited additional staffing and congressional funding.

Building upon Sheridan's recommendations, the secretary of war requested in 1886 appropriations to establish a school of instruction at Fort Riley, and the House Military Committee considered a two-hundred thousand-dollar appropriation to fund its construction. Intertwined with this process were more than military benefits and considerations. The anticipated build-up of Fort Riley offered economic opportunities for the local community. State delegations were keenly aware of the benefits the permanent military installations brought to their constituents. As a result, planned improvements at Fort Riley briefly developed into a point of contention between the Kansas and Missouri congressional delegations. Missouri congressmen were concerned that making Fort Riley the center of cavalry training might decrease the importance of Jefferson Barracks in St. Louis. Nevertheless, the House committee eventually forwarded the bill to the floor with the justification:

A school is needed for both men and horses for cavalry, and a school is needed for batteries where the range is sufficient for any caliber of piece. At Fort Riley, where this school is proposed to be located, the Government owns a reservation of over 20,000 acres of land, ample for the operation of the batteries and the cavalry, and its location favorable by reason of railway facilities, for distribution of troops upon the shortest notice to any exposed point. In an economic view, this measure is desirable, for at Riley we have wood and water in abundance, and forage and supplies can be furnished at the cheapest rates.

General Sheridan reinforced this argument in a letter to the committee stating, "the horse should be broken and the recruit instructed" at the same post.

In September 1886 Secretary of War William Endicott, anticipating congressional approval of the committee's recommendation, authorized spending forty thousand dollars to begin improvements at Fort Riley. Pond now assumed the title of constructing quartermaster and assembled a team to begin the project: John Farley became his private secretary and William Goding the architect. John Stair joined Pond's staff as the civil engineer. Coinciding with these developments, Pond advertised for bids to begin construction of additional barracks and officers' quarters.

Meanwhile, the appropriations request moved through Congress. On December 6, 1886, the House passed the bill appropriating the two hundred thousand dollars requested. The bill moved to the upper chamber where Kansas's U.S. senators Preston Plumb and John J. Ingalls assisted its passage. The next month Congress authorized money for the school and construction of quarters, barracks, and stables. While this represented a giant step toward professional training for the mounted branch of service, the *Army and Navy Journal* cautioned, "A year or two will necessarily elapse before the post will be in a condition to warrant the opening of the new school."

General Sheridan, determined to move construction along as quickly as possible, appointed a panel of officers to convene at Fort Riley. These officers surveyed the grounds, reviewed plans for quarters, barracks, and stables, and inspected sanitary conditions. In addition, they recommended quartering the cavalry and artillery on separate parts of the post. Contracts were soon awarded for installing a water and sewer system, and construction on several sets of quarters also began. Older quarters were repaired, and bathrooms were added to the hospital. Sixty paid civilian employees worked on the hospital or quarried stone from a nearby quarry.

In 1887 Congress authorized funds for additional construction at Fort Riley, including stables (top), cavalry barracks (bottom), and quarters. This appropriation represented a large step toward professional training for the mounted branch of the army. General Sheridan was determined to move construction along as quickly as possible and visited Fort Riley in the spring of 1887 to review plans and design.

Underscoring his continuing interest and involvement in the project, Sheridan visited Fort Riley in March 1887. He reviewed the board's design and agreed to locate the artillery school apart from the cavalry. Simultaneously, Captain Pond was conducting meetings, supervising the drawing of architectural plans, surveying proposed building sites, and overseeing the work already under way. In the spring of 1887 he reported:

> I have in process of construction under contracts, two double Barracks, two double Office Quarters, a set of Quarters for Hospital Steward, a system of sewers besides repairs. This work alone and more especially if I am charged with the additional construction contemplated here, will keep me busily employed.

In September 1887 the Seventh Cavalry replaced the Fifth Cavalry, which had left the post earlier that summer. The Seventh left Fort Riley nearly two decades earlier and spent most of these years staffing various frontier outposts or taking part in campaigns against the Plains Indians. The regiment returned to the post where they had been formed under the command of the late Lieutenant Colonel George A. Custer. Their commander now was Colonel James W. Forsyth, whose military career had begun before the Civil War.

Anticipating the next phase of construction and the need for congressional support, Senators Ingalls and Plumb made separate visits to Fort Riley in the fall. Plumb examined plans and toured the post with Colonel Forsyth and Captain Pond. He was impressed by the building plans, economy of construction, and architectural style. While expressing reservations about securing full funding, Plumb nevertheless stated that Fort Riley would "gradually grow into the greatest military establishment on the continent, and that as a consequence of Sheridan's ideas, Central Kansas will become a wonderful horse region."

In early November Pond traveled to Washington and presented to General Sheridan the next phase of building plans that he and architect Goding had prepared. These detailed locating the cavalry and artillery buildings so that the commanding officer's quarters would be midway between the two. Thirty-six sets of double officers' quarters would front an avenue extending toward the cavalry barracks, which would be located to give "an admirable parade ground for the cavalry." Sheridan quickly reviewed and approved the plans.

The onset of winter slowed outside construction but did not curb the moment's optimism. A reporter commented, "The spirit of progress has

James W. Forsyth graduated from the U.S. Military Academy in 1856, and his career spanned four decades. In 1886 he was promoted to colonel of the Seventh U.S. Cavalry, and he came to Fort Riley the following year. He was instrumental in initially organizing instruction for the Cavalry and Light Artillery School. Forsyth also commanded soldiers in the Battle of Wounded Knee, Dakota Territory, in December 1890.

indeed arisen from the smoldering ashes of the past, and old Riley will be one of the 'myths' of the future." Certainly a "boom" spirit permeated the civilian community in nearby Junction City. Increased federal spending and expansion of the fort benefited the local economy, which contrasted with recent downturns in other parts of the state. Articles in the *Wichita Eagle, Manhattan Mercury*, and *Hutchinson Daily News* trumpeted the benefits of improvements at the fort.

With work well under way on the quarters and barracks, attention turned to another important support building—a new hospital. In February 1888 a board of officers met to consider possible sites for its location. Originally, Pond proposed the hospital be built southeast of the future administration building. However, following the meeting he wrote, "the Post surgeon favors a General Hospital located to the N.E. of the Artillery Post." The rationale was quite simple: the northerly site further removed the hospital from the close proximity of horse stables and the river. In April the hospital contract was awarded while work continued, "providing water-closets, grease traps, house drains, etc. in connection with the new officer's quarters."

According to the secretary of war's annual report, $171,217 had been spent on the Fort Riley project during the fiscal year ending

June 30, 1888. But more appropriations were needed, and in the early months of 1888 Sheridan requested three hundred thousand dollars to continue the work. Sheridan died as Congress considered additional funding, and Senator Plumb expressed concern about whether the full amount would be approved in the current year. But when the final vote was counted, Congress authorized fifty thousand dollars more than Sheridan had requested. Meanwhile, the flurry of work continued at Fort Riley. The hospital was nearly completed, a contract had been awarded to build a consolidated mess hall, and the artillery post was under construction. By the end of 1888 fifty-five new buildings dotted the post.

In early May 1889 Redfield Proctor, the new secretary of war, and Commanding General of the Army John M. Schofield briefly visited Fort Riley and were given a tour by Pond. Pond accompanied the party to Denver, taking along maps, drawings, and estimates that he used to brief the group on present and future plans. The improvements and Fort Riley's location were already causing some army leaders to plan future regiment-scale maneuvers at the post.

Finished construction in 1889 included the academic building, four sets of quarters, a dispensary, guardhouse, two double sets of cavalry barracks with circular latrines, the heating plant and engineers' quarters, six cavalry stables, and three buildings for noncommissioned officers' quarters. On the artillery sub-post, construction included completion of the artillery administration building, two barracks, four sets of officers' quarters, and one gun shed.

One of the more important accomplishments was completion of the consolidated mess hall. This was a radical departure in the feeding of soldiers. Discarding the traditional method that required soldiers from each company to prepare the food for their mess mates, the new plan called for one mess hall with trained cooks to feed all the men. This method had been tried at recruiting depots but not on a troop-level installation. The mess hall built at Fort Riley included a large kitchen with attached bakeries and pantries that could feed up to one thousand men at one sitting. On December 4 the facility served its first meal.

A reporter for the *Kansas City Gazette* described the emerging appearance of the "new" fort:

> To the civilian the term officers' quarters as applied to these homes for the officers and their families, is a misnomer. The quarter's are handsome two story stone residences picturesquely arranged near the different posts. The single quarters for commanding and field officers contain sixteen rooms, not including kitchen and laundry. They are as well

Plans designated that the artillery school be built apart from the cavalry complex, with the commanding officer's quarters midway between. The 1895 photo (top) is of the artillery administration building. In 1888 a contract was awarded to build a consolidated mess hall (bottom). The mess hall plan discarded the traditional method that required soldiers to prepare food for their mess mates and called for one mess hall with trained cooks to feed all the men.

In April 1888 a contract was awarded for the new post hospital, which would be located northeast of the artillery school.

While construction continued, attention also was given to post beautification, and workers planted ornamental and shade trees and seeded lawns. One observer remarked, "In five years Fort Riley will be the most picturesque and beautiful spot west of the Mississippi." Landscaping efforts are evident in this photo of the administration building, also known as Regiment Hall.

finished and as conveniently arranged as the best of city residences of the same size. They are heated with steam, supplied with water from the water works, have perfect sewer connections and have every comfort and convenience known in modern civilized life. The double quarters differ from the single quarters in the fact that the buildings are arranged for two families instead of one, the house being constructed double. In each division are eight rooms with kitchen and laundry with all the conveniences spoken of above. Here the officers with their families live and enjoy life in delightful contrast with former experiences during war times or on the western frontier.

The purpose is to make an innovation at Fort Riley on a time honored practice in the army which will do away with a vast amount of shifting around among officers under certain conditions. Whenever a new officer is assigned a position at a Post, he has a choice of all the quarters occupied by officers who are his juniors. He makes his choice and the occupant must move out. He in turn has his choice from among the quarters of his juniors and he makes it and so it goes on down through the list. It frequently happens that the coming of one officer to a Post causes eight or ten officers and their families to move. The intention is to secure the adoption of a regulation which will do away with this very inconvenient practice.

Even while construction continued, attention to post beautification was considered. Workers planted ornamental and shade trees while lawns in front of many residences were "handsomely laid out and beautified and seeded." This led one observer to comment, "In five years Fort Riley will be the most picturesque and beautiful spot west of the Mississippi." These and other previous efforts at improving the landscape of the post were consistent with the nineteenth-century notion of "domesticating the wilderness."

General Sherman visited Fort Riley in mid-July 1890 with a seventeen-gun salute greeting his arrival. Considering his long advocacy of a professional and better garrisoned army, the recent improvements at Fort Riley must have been gratifying. Later that fall Secretary of War Proctor and General of the Army Schofield again visited the post to see the improvements that were making Fort Riley the talk of the army.

Recently completed buildings included two sets of field officers' quarters, two double sets of officers' quarters, the remodeled post hospital—which now served as the post headquarters—a "dead house" (morgue), and a bridge over the Kansas River. After nearly four years and expenditure of more than $1.2 million, Captain Pond could see the Fort

Riley project nearing completion. A modern post existed where the army could garrison, train, and educate light artillery and cavalry. Pond's accomplishments were cause for fireworks and celebration the following Fourth of July:

> When he began the work in August 1885 he found six sets of old officer's quarters, the same number of rickety barracks, 5 stables, an old hospital, guard house and a few unimportant buildings scattered, here and there. Plans for two posts, contemplating the expenditure of a million and a half dollars, were made and approved by the secretary of war, and the building of what will some day be the great interior military post and distributing point for the nation was commenced. Capt. Pond leaves a monument in Fort Riley that will ever stand as something to be proud of.

The *Kansas City Star* dubbed the fort "the finest military post in America, perhaps in the world."

A newly arrived sergeant wrote a friend in the weeks before Christmas 1890:

> We are here now over a week and everybody is pleased with the post and its surroundings. Our company [is] quartered in the older barracks. These are large, roomy buildings and are all that a soldier can wish for.
>
> The consolidated mess is, so far as we have seen, a great success. The food is cooked well and far better than the average company in the Army is able to provide for their men on account of not having experienced cooks. Apparently the administration and management of this large concern has been in the hands of men who understand the handling of a soldier's ration, and great credit is due the officer who has been in charge of the mess, a detail which is not sought by many and few are capable of properly filling it.

While these improvements heralded a transition of the fort's mission to a school post, the soldiers assigned to Fort Riley were called upon one last time for frontier duty against Indians. The alert came in late November 1890 in response to a rekindling of cultural values and customs among the Teton Sioux known as the Ghost Dance. The Ghost Dance religion preached by the Paiute shaman Wovoka was a call for Indian cultural renewal. For many Indians it served as an emotional and spiritual uplifting, a way to overcome their despair. The Sioux on Pine Ridge and Rosebud Reservations in South Dakota had been decimated by disease and food shortages due to corrupt reservation agents.

In 1890 Fort Riley troops moved out by train to Pine Ridge Reservation in Dakota Territory with orders to disarm a band of Indians and restore order. Shots were fired, and the ensuing bloodshed came to be known as the Wounded Knee Massacre. A burial detail later interred 146 Indians who died that day.

The agents believed the dance disrupted their agencies and cost them control. When Indians stopped going to the schools, churches, and programs that were assimilating them, the agents declared that an outbreak of violence was imminent. The secretary of the interior turned the reservations over to the military to restore order, and troops were dispatched by railroad from Fort Riley and elsewhere.

Troops of the Seventh Cavalry moved by train to Pine Ridge Reservation in Dakota Territory. When they appeared many Sioux left the reservation for the Badlands. The Fort Riley troops arrived on the scene with orders to disarm and escort a band of Indians back to the Pine Ridge Agency. The Seventh Cavalry surrounded the Sioux in Big Foot's band and trained Hotchkiss cannons on them. In the process of disarming the Indians on December 29, 1890, shots were fired. The ensuing bloodshed, where Indians and soldiers were shot, stabbed, and clubbed, came to be known as the Wounded Knee Massacre. Twenty-five soldiers were killed and forty others were wounded. Exactly how many Indians died is not known. A burial detail interred

In November 1891 a symbolic link to the Seventh Cavalry's past ended when the horse Comanche, the only survivor of Custer's command at the Battle of the Little Bighorn, died at Fort Riley from old age.

146 on the battlefield with seven others dying later from their wounds. This officially ended the Indian wars in the West.

General Nelson Miles, Commander of the Division of the Missouri, condemned Colonel Forsyth for deploying his troops in such close proximity to the Sioux. Miles also charged him with incompetence for not taking precautions against the sudden outbreak of violence. In January 1891 a court of inquiry convened and eventually cleared Forsyth of any negligence or wrongdoing. He was restored to command of the Seventh Cavalry.

In mid-January 1891 the soldiers began returning to Riley. A news account in the *Junction City Republican* reported, "The wives of the enlisted men [killed], with their little ones gathered around them, was a sad sight. Many of them were left without means when their husbands were ordered to the front, which makes it all the harder for them." The wounded were taken to the post hospital. Reflecting the prevailing attitude of the community, the *Republican* concluded, "The officers and men have performed their duties like soldiers, without hope of reward or praise, and should now be allowed a good long rest."

The routine of garrison life slowly returned. Later that summer Captain Pond left Fort Riley for a new assignment. In November a symbolic link to the Seventh Cavalry's past—the horse Comanche, the only survivor of Custer's immediate command from the Battle on the Little Bighorn—died at Fort Riley from old age. As part of their new duties, officers began developing plans and training schedules for the Cavalry and Light Artillery School. The work of the preceding six years had given new purpose to this once frontier post. The project had been the most ambitious and expensive undertaken by the army to date. Approximately $1.2 million had been expended in remodeling the post. Fort Riley was ready to assume its new mission as a school post.

9

Life at Fort Riley

On the frontier, both officers' and enlisted soldiers' lives revolved around two elements: routine and army regulations. Most soldiers joined the army hoping for excitement, to chase Indians and fire their weapons. In reality, most of their time was spent at the post, with limited time spent on actual patrol and very infrequent contact with Indians. Instead drill and guard duty, daily fatigue details, care and construction of post facilities, grooming and feeding cavalry mounts, and occasional target practice consumed their days.

In a typical day established by post orders, everything revolved around the trumpet calls.

6:00 A.M. reveille, assembly, and first roll call of troops
6:30 A.M. mess (breakfast)
7:30 A.M. fatigue call
8:00 A.M. sick call
9:00 A.M. assembly of guard detail
9:45 A.M. recall from fatigue details
10:00–11:30 A.M. various drills for infantry, artillery, and cavalry
12:00 NOON mess
1:00 P.M. target practice drill
2:00 P.M. additional fatigue call
4:30 P.M. recall from fatigue duties
6:00 P.M. mess

9:00 P.M. tattoo, assembly of troops, and last roll call
9:30 P.M. taps, lights out

This routine varied at each post but was the essential structure of the day's activities, even with most of the garrison absent on detached duty during the summer.

The bane of a soldier's life was fatigue detail. Rather than firing weapons, soldiers spent more time shouldering an ax or shovel because using enlisted personal for construction and maintenance work was less expensive than hiring civilians. Even when civilian employees worked at Fort Riley during the many stages of construction, troops performed most of the heavy labor. At least these soldiers were eligible for additional pay of twenty-five cents a day. Fatigue details took many forms. Soldiers assigned to the mess chopped wood for stoves and carried water for the cooks. They also washed dishes, set tables before meals, and waited on their peers while they ate. A frequent assignment for privates was to police (clean up) the grounds. Cavalry units stationed at Fort Riley had the additional duty of stable service, requiring them to clean and groom their mounts and to clean up after them. Stable service must be completed before the cavalry ate, much to the amusement of infantry and artillery companies. The Kansas frontier also created other tasks: soldiers at Fort Riley frequently found themselves pulling sunflowers out of the parade ground. Needless to say, soldiers disliked fatigue duty and resented the amount of time they spent on these tasks. However, once the tasks were completed a soldier's time was his own. Army regulations required soldiers be within hearing distance of bugle calls on the post, unless given permission to leave the area.

Food at Fort Riley and other frontier posts was no more exciting than the daily routine. The government provided daily rations of beans, hardtack, salt bacon, coffee, flour, range beef, coffee beans, and coarse bread based on the number of men officially on company rolls. Salt, brown sugar, and molasses were provided either to cover up or add to the taste of the food. Prepared and eaten in company messes, most foods were boiled together no matter what their original form, leading to a variety of stews, hashes, and dishes referred to as "slumgullions." Whenever possible this menu was supplemented by freshly hunted buffalo, deer, or fish. However, Surgeon Isaac Coates and others observed that officers often reserved the right to hunt for themselves when at the post and as a result ate better than their men.

Missing from these menus and diets were vegetables, milk, eggs, butter, and fresh fruit. The need for fresh produce to fight scurvy was well

Daily routine consumed much of a soldier's time, which among other duties included caring for the cavalry horses.

known, but the quartermaster's and civilian government's concern with transportation costs prevented frontier forts being supplied with these needed items. Enlisted men had to acquire them in nearby communities such as Junction City, purchase them from the post sutler, or grow them. Since most companies did not have as many men on their rosters as the official records show, they had surplus government issue supplies to trade for fresh foods or sell for cash, which was then placed in the company mess fund. Companies spent the cash for fresh vegetables, dairy products, spices, turkeys, and fresh fruits. Sergeant Samuel Evans of the Seventh Cavalry credited his F Company mess fund for their superior dining at Fort Riley in 1888.

The government and post surgeons encouraged growing gardens at every frontier post. From the army's standpoint, raising fresh vegetables at each local post saved transportation costs and improved the men's health. It encouraged both general post and individual company gardens. Designated company gardeners were excused from other fatigue duties, and enlisted men generally did not complain about assignments to the garden areas. Friendly rivalry between units was encouraged. More established posts like Fort Riley could grow impressive gardens. However, with frequent troop departures removing gardeners, inclement weather, and plagues of grasshoppers, the gardens often suffered.

Soldiers' leisure time was sometimes spent at neighboring Junction City where many vices such as gambling, alcohol, and prostitution were available.

One of the most popular military truisms is that soldiers have few rights, but one of them is the right to complain. Troops stationed at frontier posts found several things to complain about including pay, clothing, discipline, and the previously mentioned fatigue duties. Pay for a private at Fort Riley ranged from a low of eleven dollars per month when the post was established in 1853 to a high of sixteen dollars per month under Civil War pay guidelines. In 1870 the government reduced the monthly pay to thirteen dollars per month, and a wave of desertions followed. Civilian employees at Fort Riley were earning as much as thirty dollars per month, while other laborers were paid $1.25 per day. Troopers reasoned that if civilian workers earned more each month, why not desert and take advantage of these opportunities? Cavalrymen deserting often took their mounts and other equipment, thus increasing the loss and cost to the government.

Army regulations called for the paymaster to visit every two months, but this regularly stretched to four or six months on the frontier. When he did arrive, the troops would queue up by company, in order of seniority. Payday was important to the men and for the local economy. The weekly *Junction City Union* happily announced when "the Paymaster at Fort Riley is distributing greenbacks." Recently paid troops bought fresh foods, presents, and tobacco, and they lost money gambling and visiting prostitutes in nearby Junction City.

Discipline could be harsh. Army regulations left most punishments to the discretion of the commanding officer, or if formally charged, to the ranking officer of the court. Soldiers could be whipped, forced to march carrying their saddles and other equipment for hours in a hot sun, jailed with only bread or water to eat, or anything else a creative commander could assign. Since these punishments occurred for such infractions as laughing in ranks or failing to clean a saddle properly, many soldiers complained that they were too harsh.

But post commanders also had to cope with serious problems. Besides desertion, the frontier army fought a battle with drinking and alcoholism. Not all soldiers drank irresponsibly, but too often officers faced the problem described by former Sergeant Percival Lowe, who believed that 10 percent of his company was regularly in the guardhouse for crimes committed while drunk. Some post commanders tried to keep alcohol off the posts, while others organized temperance societies on the base. The first such society was organized for both Fort Riley and near-by Junction City in 1857. Ironically, fighting the problem became more difficult after President Rutherford B. Hayes issued an executive order in 1881 forbidding the sale of whiskey on all military establishments. This forced troops to frequent the "hog ranches" off post, where they lost their pay to gamblers, drank watered whiskey, and visited diseased prostitutes. Soldiers from Fort Riley spent their time and money similarly in Junction City.

The army careers of most soldiers ended peacefully. Some like Private John Radley mustered out in 1854 and stayed to work for the post quartermaster. Others built homesteads in the Solomon, Smoky Hill, or Republican River valleys. Most soldiers however, accepted the army's offer to transport them back to the city where they enlisted.

Of course the regulars and volunteers were not the only occupants of Fort Riley during these years. Wives and families also lived on the post. The army acknowledged that women exercised a good moral influence on the men, and their presence boosted the morale of troops in general. However, as Elizabeth Custer indignantly observed, army regulations did not officially recognize their presence at the post. Only camp laundresses were officially recognized; all other women, wives, and children were lumped under the designation of "camp followers." Laundresses, often the wives of enlisted men, were assigned quarters, awarded daily rations, and offered the services of the post surgeon. Married enlisted men had the special privilege of eating and sleeping away from the company mess and barracks. Officers received extra

Wives and families of soldiers at times lived on the post. Women, it was believed, exercised good moral influences on the men. Possibly the most well-known army wife was Elizabeth Custer, who made her home at Fort Riley while her husband, George A. Custer, was there and in the field with the Seventh Cavalry.

money for "table pay" (additional food allowance for married officers) but had to cover other costs of their family's existence out of their own pockets. Other women on base included cooks and servants for officers' wives. Some of these servants were already wives of enlisted men; the unmarried were quickly pursued by and married to others on the post. Enlisted men could only marry with permission of their commanding officer. Because of their low pay, their wives needed to work as laundresses or governesses to make ends meet.

Officers' quarters were assigned or chosen by rank and seniority. Any higher ranking officer could select quarters already occupied and require the occupants to move. This process was referred to as "ranking out." The officer and family evicted in this way then visited the same favor on a lower ranking staffer. Quarters could be made into areas for parties, or left quite austere, depending on the occupants. Elizabeth Custer (Libbie to her friends) accompanied her husband to his new assignment at Fort Riley in 1866. She wrote to a cousin, "Our house is so comfortable and cheery for we have sunlight in the parlor all day." The quarters were roomy, with carpeted bedrooms and a walk-in dressing room. They also had a large parlor for entertaining. Libbie's presence, along with that of other officers' wives, contributed to a sense of sociability and civility. In a letter written shortly after her arrival, she recorded attending an officer's bachelor party, "a pleasant affair and more than that, quite gay." The following week she hosted a party for the officers of the garrison because her quarters had a large kitchen and dining room. Even though local sutler John Price offered groceries and other provisions on post, Libbie shopped at stores in the small but growing town of Junction City. There she purchased boiled hams, turkeys, coffee, champagne, cake, and nuts for the meal. The Custers quickly settled into their quarters.

Holidays were special for everyone at Fort Riley and other frontier garrisons. On days such as Christmas, Independence Day, Thanksgiving, and Washington's Birthday most regular duties were suspended. Holidays meant celebrating with parties, games, parades, and other events. Christmas celebrations were planned far in advance, with company mess funds spent for special treats and surprises. Commanders often released prisoners in the guardhouse to enjoy the holiday. Officers and enlisted men, who normally socialized in separate circles, altered the rules on special days. It was customary for an officer to spend part of the day celebrating with his company, usually in the mess hall.

The Fourth of July caused the greatest revelry and celebration. Such was certainly the case at Fort Riley from its earliest years. The approach of the Fourth of July 1854 caused soldiers and workers to plan a celebration. They made a private agreement with an individual off post—perhaps the Dixon brothers—to have 150 gallons of whiskey and ten gallons of wine delivered secretly to a spot near Three Mile Creek, east of main post. Several days before the revelry, the goods were duly received and sampled by a private. As the last keg was rolled into the brush, a sergeant and two soldiers appeared and arrested the entire party. Fearing the consequences, the private threw himself on the ground and begged for mercy. The teamster supplying the contraband proposed to give the sergeant ten dollars, and in turn the kegs would be destroyed. The sergeant refused the bribe and commenced to knock in the heads of the kegs. Taking note of this, the civilian quickly made his exit, glad to have escaped without being officially detained. But the story did not end there. The enterprising sergeant saved the liquor and sold it for a dollar a quart, and according to one report, "the Fourth of July was celebrated in a lively manner."

The official observance included the reading of the Declaration of Independence by Dr. William Hammond, who became surgeon general

Marriages were special occasions at the fort. The social event of 1855 was the marriage of Flora Cooke, daughter of Colonel Philip St. George Cooke, to the handsome Lieutenant J.E.B. Stuart.

of the United States during the Civil War. Appropriate remarks were offered by several officers. Following this, an opportunity was given for anyone to speak. A young, newly arrived recruit stepped forward and, according to one account, made the best speech of the day. Other years would see horse races, baseball games, shooting competitions, and fireworks. When a regimental band was stationed at the post, they would play for the assembled troops and families.

Marriages also were special occasions at the fort. The social event of 1855 was the marriage of Lieutenant Colonel Philip St. George Cooke's daughter Flora to a handsome young lieutenant of the First Cavalry, J.E.B. Stuart. He had just returned from providing mail escort duty. Stuart, like his soon to be father-in-law, was a native Virginian. He was young, handsome, and had graduated from West Point in June 1854. The wedding probably took place in the commanding officer's quarters at Fort Riley on November 14 and may have been attended by Colonel Robert E. Lee and Lieutenant Colonel Albert Sydney Johnston. Flora wore her white school graduation dress, and the newlyweds traveled to Fort Leavenworth the next day to set up housekeeping.

When not on duty in the fort or on patrol, a soldier's time was his own. He soon discovered that off-duty companionship was linked to the men of his company. This was especially true for cavalry and infantry outfits, which had little social contact with each other. A much larger social chasm existed between officers and enlisted men. Officers and their wives and families socialized together; enlisted men and their families did the same. The well established social structure was observed by both adults and children. Officers' wives quickly learned that horseback riding was the most popular form of recreation available to them. They could ice skate and go sleighing during the winter. Wives could have year-round reading circles and sewing bees, both utilized as forums for socializing, news exchanges, and completing projects. Social life always picked up during the winter after troops returned from summer campaigns. With their husbands at home, wives hosted dinner or card parties. Jennie Barnitz, wife of Major Albert Barnitz, Seventh Cavalry, and Surgeon Isaac Coates both praised the parties given by Libbie Custer at Fort Riley in late winter of 1867. Both the quality of the food and the topic of discussion by both men and women present—Indian wars and massacres—surprised the attendees.

During the evenings officers might gather for cards or other entertainment or simply to enjoy their tobacco as they discussed their chosen profession of arms. In the 1850s such gatherings were chaired by Colonel Philip St. George Cooke, the old dragoon and cavalry tactician. One of his students, Captain John Buford, would gain greater fame as the Union officer who defined the initial federal battle lines at the small Pennsylvania village of Gettysburg. Lieutenant J.E.B. Stuart spent his spare time creating his "lightning horse hitcher," designed to speed a cavalryman mounting his horse. He also created the "Stuart's Saber Attachment" during the winter of 1858–1859, which mounted the saber on the saddle. Stuart received a patent for that invention, which the army adopted. Captain Nathaniel Lyon's daily account book provides insight into his personal affairs and interests. He spent evenings enjoying his favorite game, billiards, and kept a constant supply of cigars. Summer afternoons found him frequenting the post sutler's store to enjoy a cool beer. He also had a sweet tooth, purchasing sweets in one- and two-pound quantities on a monthly basis.

For enlisted men living in the barracks without families the principal recreation was visiting and talking. Beyond that all soldiers had to improvise, as the nineteenth-century army did little to provide rest and recreation opportunities. Cavalry outfits at Fort Riley held horse races. Soldiers sang for pleasure in the barracks, including popular folk tunes, old Civil War ballads, and some songs specifically complaining about the

Recreation at Fort Riley was limited but at times included horse races, variety shows, and theatrical performances. Musical entertainment, such as that provided by the Sixth Cavalry Band, pictured here, offered evenings of enjoyment at social hops and suppers.

rigors of army life. Variety and minstrel shows were popular. Some shows traveled from Kansas City and St. Louis to Fort Riley. When professionals were not available, the troops created their own amateur entertainments The winter months of 1872–1873 witnessed a revival in theatrical performances on post, with soldiers, wives, and children taking part. Organized the preceding winter, the Fort Riley Theatrical Association performed in a totally renovated building. In an effort to attract more civilians from Junction City, a sergeant ran his hack, or horse and buggy, to town. The season closed in March and was termed a success. The Sixth Cavalry Band members also provided evenings of entertainment in their barracks with social hops and suppers. Such performances were quite common when bands were stationed at regimental headquarters.

Social clubs and various orders were established on bases. A Masonic Lodge was organized in 1857, with the first meeting held in the quarters of the newly promoted Captain Lewis Armistead. Some soldiers gambled in the barracks and off the military reservation. Army regulations officially forbade any forms of gambling on the post, but as a rule officers broke up only high-stakes games. Other popular recreations included drinking and visiting prostitutes at hog ranches. The army tried to cut down on excessive drinking because drunken soldiers were unable to perform their duties, and drunks were bad for discipline. A growing temperance movement in the army led the International Order of Good Templars to establish temperance branches on posts such as Fort Riley and in nearby communities. But to many regulars the adage "good fighters are often good drinkers" remained the rule, and the occasional spree did not mark a soldier as a heavy and problem drinker.

The army reorganization act that created the Seventh, Eighth, Ninth, and Tenth Cavalry regiments in 1866 also required that school facilities be established for enlisted men at all permanent posts. Sometimes the post commander appointed the chaplain to run the school, which is how Chaplain Charlie Reynolds became the teacher at Fort Riley during the 1860s. If not the chaplain, the post commander assigned an educated soldier this task, and he received an additional thirty-five cents per day. As per army regulations the curriculum included basic reading, writing, mathematics, and a little geography and history. For the soldiers who entered the army unable to read or write, the school provided an opportunity to learn skills they could use later in civilian life. Larger posts such as Fort Riley eventually established libraries. Soldiers contributed pay to enable the library to order regional newspapers such as the *Kansas City Times* and national press such as the *New York Herald* and the *New York Tribune*. Private Martin Anderson, a Danish immigrant, declared that "my recreation was mostly in the Fort Riley library studying. I spent most of my spare time to learn English."

Health care was a serious concern at Fort Riley and other frontier outposts. Some forts were assigned regular army surgeons or paid civilian doctors; more isolated outposts survived without either. Isaac Coates was hired by the army on March 7, 1867, to serve as assistant surgeon for "$100 per month, or $113.83 when performing services in the field." The salaries reflect the early focus on wounds and combat injuries. Officials gave little emphasis to personal hygiene, preventative medicine, or sanitation except in times of crisis such as threatened cholera outbreaks. This primitive state of medical care led to a high rate of sickness from cholera, dysentery, and venereal disease. The average soldier was hospitalized three times per year, and one out of every thirty-three died of disease. Among the troops at Fort Riley cholera caused more deaths than did combat, and outbreaks of diphtheria and influenza were common.

The quality of health care at Fort Riley, including the application of preventative medicine, improved with each decade. The new post hospital boosted the post surgeon's efforts, and the commitment of several

Bernard John Dowling Irwin served as the post surgeon at Fort Riley on two different occasions in the late 1860s and early 1870s. His efforts during the campaign against the Chiricahua Indians in Arizona Territory on the eve of the Civil War eventually earned him the Medal of Honor.

talented and far-sighted post surgeons contributed to the improvements between 1866 and 1873. During this time the post surgeon was a commissioned officer and usually held the rank of major. His responsibilities were second in importance only to those of post commander. The post surgeon focused his attention on the recurring issues of post sanitation while ensuring the garrison's health.

The first notable post surgeon was Bernard J. D. Irwin who arrived at Fort Riley in April 1866. A native of Ireland, Irwin was educated in New York and Vermont. He entered army medical service in 1856 and served on the frontier. This service included involvement in a battle against Apaches near Apache Pass, Arizona Territory, in February 1861, for which he eventually was awarded the Congressional Medal of Honor.

Surgeon George M. Sternberg succeeded Irwin. He had served at other frontier Kansas forts and lost his wife during the 1867 cholera epidemic at Fort Harker. In the fall of 1867 he arrived at Fort Riley and, with the exception of a few months, remained at Riley until April 1870. Sternberg became a brilliant bacteriologist and epidemiologist and later served as surgeon general of the army. He also had an interest in and knack for inventing devices. To maintain an even temperature in hospi-

George M. Sternberg succeeded Irwin as post surgeon. He had previously served at other frontier forts and had exhaustingly fought the 1867 cholera epidemic at Fort Harker. After losing his wife to the disease, he came to Fort Riley in the fall of 1867 where he remained, with the exception of a few months, until 1870. He later served as surgeon general of the army.

tal wards, he created an automatic heat regulator based on a thermometer that made and broke an electric circuit.

Sternberg was constantly vigilant, looking after the health and welfare of the troops. In a letter to the post adjutant in June 1869, he admonished:

> as soon as practicable arrangements may be made to enable the soldiers of each company at the Post, to bathe themselves as often as once a week at or near their quarters. For this purpose a special room should be provided for each company, with bathtubs and facilities for obtaining water. The half of a pork barrel would answer very well for a bathtub, two or three buckets of water in such a tub would enable a man to take a very satisfactory bath and with six tubs a whole company would probably be able to bathe between Retreat on Saturday night and Inspection on Sunday morning.

He concluded this would be preferable to the men bathing in the river. Monthly inspections, so important for monitoring and maintaining a healthy command, sometimes uncovered unusual medical issues. After

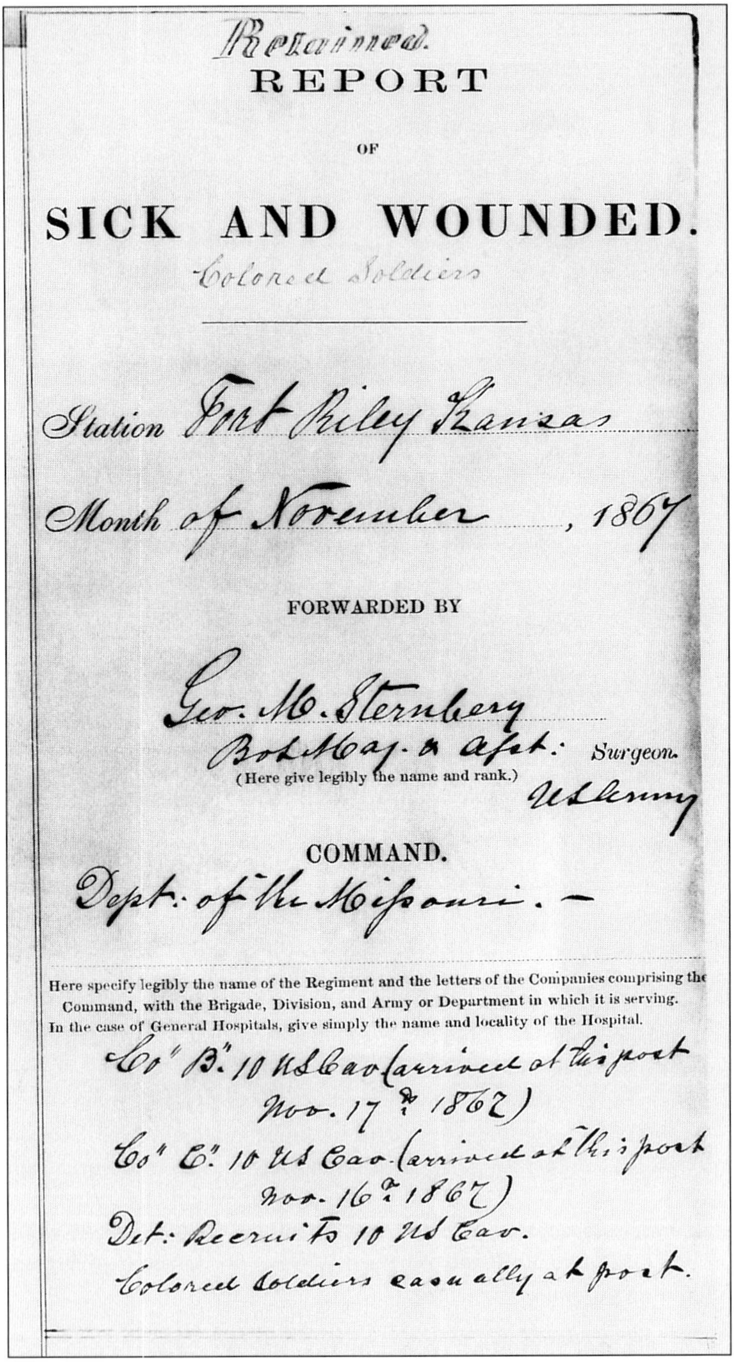

REPORT

OF

SICK AND WOUNDED.

Colored Soldiers

Station *Fort Riley Kansas*

Month *of November*, *1867*

FORWARDED BY

Geo. M. Sternberg
Bvt. Maj. & asst. Surgeon.
(Here give legibly the name and rank.)
US Army

COMMAND.

Dept. of the Missouri. —

Here specify legibly the name of the Regiment and the letters of the Companies comprising the
Command, with the Brigade, Division, and Army or Department in which it is serving.
In the case of General Hospitals, give simply the name and locality of the Hospital.

Co" B". 10 US Cav (arrived at this post
Nov. 17th 1867)
Co" C". 10 US Cav. (arrived at this post
Nov. 16th 1867)
Det: Recruits 10 US Cav.
Colored Soldiers casually at post.

Fort Riley medical report, issued in 1867 and signed by surgeon George M. Sternberg.

116

one inspection Sternberg admonished an officer that the company's pig pen was too close to the company barracks. He instructed another commander to clean up a garbage pile outside the barracks.

Sternberg also considered the physical condition of buildings and their affect on soldiers. He echoed the sentiments of an earlier report that described the guardhouse as "totally unfitted for its purpose." Sternberg found the structure badly ventilated "as to render the air very foul and unhealthy overnight; these, with the only one room of sufficient size, are entirely inadequate to contain the average number of prisoners, say 35; at times this number has been increased to 60, for a short time, as after pay day." A solution, which went beyond health care and addressed certain moral issues, was to divide prisoners into three classes because the "comparative boy . . . should [not] be thrown into the same cell as the hardened villain who may have served three or four years in a penitentiary and is to serve an equal number of years in a guard house of the Army."

Plans to improve the hospital probably resulted from Dr. Irwin's ideas. He reported the present building to be "dreary, forlorn, dilapidated. . . . Decay, ruin and general neglect are the marked features." In the spring of 1871 plans were approved to remodel and improve the sanitation conditions of the hospital. Construction during the following spring transformed the main ground-floor section into a single hospital ward and added a new second floor. Such an effort enhanced the overall capability of the post to provide care to soldiers. Work on the building continued while three companies of the Sixth Cavalry were in the field on summer campaign. Completion of the construction coincided with the troops' return in late October.

The weekly *Junction City Union* reported on the general post improvements. The writer indicated the post quartermaster officer was

> fixing up things generally. . . . The yards have been robbed of their luxurious crops of weeds, and put in apple-pie order. The new walks have been built. The old back porches have been refloored and inclosed, making an addition of one room to a house; the walls and rooms and halls have been painted a beautiful tint; and things have been brushed up generally, until it doesn't appear such a very great act of self-sacrifice to be an officer stationed at a fort. Altogether, Fort Riley looks at its best.

That a yearly sum be appropriated for military post repair appeared in the secretary of war's annual reports.

Close ties, if not always happy ones, describe the relations among Fort Riley and its neighbors. Federal expenditures from the fort pumped money into the economies of Davis and Riley Counties, promoting the growth of local elites in both Manhattan and Junction City. When the post advertised contracts for hay, corn, and oats local bidders were favored. During its first two years Fort Riley employed more than 30 percent of all adult males in the two counties.

The soldiers also made connections within the surrounding communities. Troopers such as Sergeant Robert Henderson claimed homesteads in river bottoms near the fort and planned to remain in the community after their enlistments expired. Lieutenant J.E.B. Stuart helped raise funds for the Episcopal church in Junction City, and both he and Captain Nathaniel Lyon had numerous business and real estate investments in the area. This symbiotic relationship was evident in bad times as well as good. Military authorities did not ignore the hardships visited upon the local and area economy. In the spring of 1875 the army responded to civilian sufferings by ordering six boxcars of excess property and rations be shipped to Fort Riley for distribution to needy civilians. Military blankets, overcoats, and shoes were handed out to the destitute of Davis and Sedgwick Counties. Further evidence of these humanitarian measures occurred when post chaplain Charles Reynolds oversaw the transport and distribution of eighteen thousand rations to Cowley County.

The concerns of daily life, completing assigned tasks, raising a family, and making ends meet occupied most of the time in a soldier's day, just as these issues did for civilians in nearby communities. Daily duties required the soldier's attention, but he had much free time as well. How soldiers spent their cash and free time in Junction City and elsewhere was part of the community ties Fort Riley developed in the region.

10

The Twentieth Century

In 1890 the superintendent of the U.S. Census Bureau declared in a bulletin that "Up to and including 1880 the country had a frontier of settlement, but at present the unsettled area has been so broken into . . . that there can hardly be said to be a frontier line." Why had the frontier period ended? Most Indians had been forced to relocate on reservations, and 8.5 million whites lived on their former hunting grounds. Railroads crisscrossed the Trans-Mississippi West, and nearly all of the farmable land was claimed. Towns and people dotted the West with signs of "civilization," including schools and churches. After 1890 the American people would have to manage their lives and economy in a closed-space world rather than on open frontiers. Both contemporaries and historians recognized that army posts such as Fort Riley were the nucleus of settlement. They adapted through the years as frontier needs changed. How would Fort Riley fare in a post-frontier era?

As the army entered the last decade of the nineteenth century, many of its leaders focused on enlisting and creating a more professional force. Settlement of the frontier, subjugation of Native American tribes, and faster means of communication and travel altered operational considerations that had dictated army strategy since the founding of the republic. During the last two decades of the century the army closed a majority of the posts that served as vanguards settling the continent's interior. In Kansas only Forts Riley and Leavenworth remained open. Throughout Fort Riley's existence, the question of maintaining

Fort Riley in 1895. During the previous decade many improvements had been made to the post as it assumed its new role as host to the Cavalry and Light Artillery School. In the center of the picture is the post chapel, completed in 1861. Within the next three years, a larger chapel would be erected to accommodate the post's spiritual needs. The new officers' quarters line (Forsyth Avenue), and in the distance the bell tower of the administration building, add further definition to a changing landscape.

a peacetime army was always connected to issues of cost and manpower concentration. Now that the army's role as Plains constabulary drew to a close, military planners had to reconsider these issues.

Why had Fort Riley remained open? Its central location, railroad connections, and lower expenses resulted in General Sherman selecting Fort Riley to be one of the large, permanent posts for the twentieth century. Sherman's decision, along with the establishment of the cavalry and artillery schools at Fort Riley, led to the federal government investing more than $1.2 million in improvements between 1885 and 1891 alone.

The company remained the basic unit of army organization, but with consolidation the regiment increasingly became important as a unit of organization and function. Regiments of one thousand to twelve hundred men (and later divisions of ten thousand to twelve thousand men) were assigned to a post for approximately three years and were then rotated. The concentration of thousands of soldiers instead of the

As the army prepared to enter a new century, efforts were made to improve the quality of life for enlisted soldiers. Barracks life, depicted here in ca. 1895, afforded the opportunity to form bonds of friendship that also fostered esprit de corps and unit loyalty. Soldiers passed their free time playing cards or shooting billiards at the post sutler's. Social and dramatic clubs also were organized to foster a sense of belonging and offer avenues for constructive activities.

hundreds of company strength dictated the need to upgrade barracks, quarters, and other support buildings. The War Department viewed military reservations with sufficient land and proximity to railheads as facilities worth maintaining. Concentrating larger bodies of troops at such locations reduced supply costs. Large reservations permitted units to train together in greater numbers and in situations similar to actual combat as well as be able to respond quickly to trouble spots. This included helping railroads suppress job actions by their workers: troops from Fort Riley were dispatched to St. Louis during the Great Railroad Strike in 1877, and they were shipped to Chicago in response to the Pullman Strike of 1894.

The Cavalry and Light Artillery School was established at Fort Riley in March 1892 with Colonel James W. Forsyth named its first commandant. This hardened campaigner believed theoretical instruction should accompany drill and practice. Instruction would be for a twelve-month duration with the final three months set aside for combined maneuvers.

Taken on the cavalry parade field between 1893 and 1897, this photo shows three troops of the Second U.S. Cavalry in parade dress uniforms. Providing training for cavalry regiments continued to be a key goal for Fort Riley into the twentieth century, as was training for its counterpart, the artillery, depicted on the facing page.

The concept called for training to be conducted by all regimental companies stationed at Fort Riley.

From the beginning, emergencies and unforeseen commitments disrupted the school's routine. For example, midway through its first year the Third Cavalry was ordered to service along the Cherokee Strip in Oklahoma Territory, interrupting its training. The outbreak of hostilities with Spain in the spring of 1898 again disrupted the school's course of instruction as cavalry troops mobilized for war. This left a skeleton detachment at the post to look after public buildings and property. During the summer of 1900 the Boxer Rebellion in China resulted in deployment of additional cavalry troops to the Far East. For all practical purposes, the school ceased instruction until the fall of 1901. While manpower and mission concerns continually interrupted the training schedule, the army nevertheless continued its commitment to the plan of making Fort Riley a center of cavalry instruction.

The new century witnessed more radical changes to the organizational structure and training of the army. This stemmed partly from army operational deficiencies discovered during the Spanish–American

Gun drill by Company F of the Second Artillery, 1896.

War. Secretary of War Eliu Root designated Fort Riley as a national encampment for war games and maneuvers in 1901, allowing for as many as thirty thousand participants. The army held joint maneuvers in the fall of 1902 between seven thousand regular and National Guard soldiers. The following year witnessed another maneuver camp—this time for Kansas troops. The post was selected to host the regional and army-wide rifle matches. Large fatigue details were organized to construct a new rifle range and support the competition in the Republican Flats, the area known today as Camp Forsyth.

Beginning with the 1903–1904 school year the first systematic instruction for officers and enlisted men was instituted. This included formation in January 1903 of a school for farriers. The following year the school added an equitation department for student officers. A school for cooks and bakers began in February 1905. These and other changes to the curriculum were improvements that Brigadier General Edward Godfrey instituted during his three-year tenure as commandant. Before his departure in October 1907 Godfrey had made significant changes to the school, which created a more progressive curriculum.

Change also involved the school's name, which became the Mounted Service School. Believing that previous work had been too experimental and post facilities were underutilized, Godfrey concluded, "A crying need in our service is a system of equitation and a school of instruction where that system can be properly exemplified and taught, and its

123

In 1901 the secretary of war designated Fort Riley a national encampment for war games and maneuvers. Here Iowa National Guard troops bivouac on the Fort Riley reservation during 1906 maneuvers.

graduates distributed throughout the mounted service to become instructors of others." This was a radical departure from the past. Previously, training at the school involved only the cavalry and artillery regiments already stationed at Fort Riley. The new plan called for officers and enlisted men from units army-wide to come to Fort Riley for training. Following the completion of their studies, they would return to their respective units.

Another significant change to the fort's mission occurred in the summer of 1906 when the army designated Fort Riley as a regimental post. This decision was an outgrowth of a plan to further economize and streamline the army's organizational structure. Once again, as throughout the fort's history, factors relating to Fort Riley's selection included its central location, having an adequate rail system to enable troop deployment, and possessing a large maneuver area. This latter consideration led to joint maneuvers at Fort Riley between National Guard and regular troops later that summer and again in 1908 and 1911.

The outbreak of two wars, one a civil war in Mexico in 1911 and the other between the major powers of Europe in the summer of 1914, again altered Fort Riley's teaching role, changes dictated once more by the

When the United States entered the European war in 1917, Fort Riley assumed a new role of wartime training center. In this 1917 photo, soldiers are engaged in a bayonet drill.

fort's central location and large military reservation. Regular and National Guard troops were ordered to take up stations in Texas and New Mexico and protect border settlements from disruptions caused by the Mexican Revolution. Fort Riley became a transit point for many units.

With the entrance of the United States into the European war in April 1917, Fort Riley assumed a new role built partly upon its utilization during the preceding decade—that of a wartime training center. Operation of the Mounted Service School was cut back drastically as the post focused on a war-time mission of training soldiers. In June the War Department selected the fort as a site for a medical officers training camp and as one of sixteen divisional cantonments to prepare recruits for eventual deployment to the fighting in France. Raw troops from Nebraska, South Dakota, Wyoming, and Missouri assembled in the largest training camp in the United States. The basic training camp was on a two-thousand-acre tract on the extreme eastern edge of the reservation known as Ogden Flats, near the former Pawnee townsite. Projected troop strength of this camp was estimated at thirty to fifty thousand soldiers.

The army named the camp Funston in honor of Kansan native Major General Frederick Funston who commanded the Twentieth Kansas Infantry in the Philippines during the Insurrection. Major General Leonard Wood became the camp's commander. French, British, and Russian officers were brought in to prepare the "doughboys" for eventual deployment on the western front, and training focused on the horrors of trench warfare.

A unique aspect of Camp Funston was an area known as the Zone of Camp Activities, commonly referred to as Army City. This four-block long area was financed and built with private capital and provided soldiers with recreational and other facilities including theaters and an arcade with refreshment booths, general merchandise stores, a fifty-chair barber shop, a seventy-table pool hall, library, and society buildings housing the YMCA, Knights of Columbus, and a YWCA Hostess House.

The same deadly outbreak of influenza that struck worldwide interrupted training at Camp Funston twice during 1918. The first cases in March 1918 sent 1,907 soldiers to hospital facilities; 50 died. The second and far more serious epidemic began in mid-September and lasted until early November. During this period the camp recorded 16,983 cases of influenza and pneumonia. Of these, 841 died. The worst day of the epidemic occurred on October 4 when 1,270 men reported to sick call. During this month the entire state of Kansas was under quarantine, and soldiers were denied passes to leave the post. Commanding General Leonard Wood declared that the troops at Fort Riley suffered more deaths than some units going into combat.

After World War I Fort Riley faced more traditional challenges, namely an economy-minded Congress advocating military cuts and a renewed emphasis on a school to prepare future military leaders. Military planners highly endorsed combined tactical education and training.The Mounted Service School was renamed the Cavalry School in the fall of 1919, and its mission was to produce balanced officers and cavalrymen who could meet tactical situations and ride well. The Cavalry Equipment Board, the mounted arms office that tested and developed new equipment, also moved to Fort Riley.

Technological advances of the First World War such as the tank, machine gun, and airplane raised fundamental questions during the 1920s and 1930s about the cavalry's future role. Citing budget constraints, the army reduced the size of the regular cavalry by almost 50 percent in 1921 and cut funding throughout the decade. Lack of funds, high ranking traditionalists' unwillingness to experiment with mecha-

Camp Funston was one of sixteen divisional training camps established after the United States entered World War I. During the summer and fall of 1917, more than fourteen hundred wooden buildings were constructed to accommodate arriving recruits. Major General Leonard Wood commanded the camp. In the spring of 1918 the Eighty-ninth Division deployed from Camp Funston to France. Eventually, more than fifty thousand "doughboys," including the Tenth Division and elements of the Ninety-second Division, also trained here.

nization, and their general suspicion of armored forces further isolated the mounted branch of the army. Over their objections several cavalry regiments reluctantly exchanged their horses for combat vehicles during the 1930s. For example, in 1937 the Thirteenth Cavalry joined the First Cavalry to form the mechanized Seventh Cavalry Brigade. The following year maneuvers were held at Fort Riley and for the first time mechanized cavalry were pitted against horse cavalry. In preparation for this exercise, the Seventh Cavalry Brigade motor "marched" from Fort Knox to Fort Riley. These and subsequent maneuvers at Fort Riley in 1938 proved the mechanical horse could replace the four-footed model and still perform the traditional cavalry missions: reconnaissance and patrol.

The growing prospect of war refocused attention on Fort Riley as a training and deployment center. In the fall of 1940 the War Department authorized a Cavalry Replacement Training Center to be constructed on flat, sandy ground adjacent to the banks of the Republican River and near the National Range. Surrounding the site were hills, canyons, gorges, and jungle thickets—a geographic diversity ideal for training a versatile soldier.

To enhance the fort's capabilities to train and to afford maneuver space for these troops, the army annexed 32,370 acres in the spring of 1941. This expansion—the first enlargement of the post since its establishment—increased the reservation's size to nearly fifty-three thousand acres. Camp Funston was rebuilt, and the Second Cavalry Division was assigned there in December 1940. This division was the first integrated army division. The all-white Second and Fourteenth Cavalry regiments joined the all-black Ninth and Tenth Cavalry regiments to form the division. During World War II nearly 125,000 trainees completed training at Fort Riley and deployed overseas as replacements.

As soldiers trained and deployed, higher command selected the fort for yet another project in 1943. Thousands of German prisoners of war, captured at the defeat of Rommel's Afrika Korps, were shipped to the United States. Fort Riley became one of thirteen camps in Kansas selected to maintain a POW camp. The Fort Riley camp had a capacity for one thousand men and occupied a small portion of Camp Funston. The prisoners were largely used for labor details to relieve the manpower shortages around the post and on farms in the area.

After World War II the fort faced reassessment. A post-war utilization study conducted by the Office of the Chief of Engineers in September 1945 concluded that Fort Riley satisfied the army's future needs. But the future did not include the traditional horse cavalry. The Cavalry School ceased operation in November 1946 and was replaced by the Ground General School. Workers converted limestone stables into office buildings, the impressive collections of manuals in the Cavalry School Library were destroyed, and other mementoes of fort's cavalry tradition disappeared. The new Ground General School instructed all newly commissioned army officers in such common courses as map reading, company administration, and military law. Following this course, lieutenants proceeded to their branch specialty schools. The school also offered correspondence courses. In addition, Fort Riley operated the army's only officers candidate school. The class lasted five and a half months and provided basic instruction for officers before they received their commissions and assignments to regular units. This school operated until July 1953 and produced more than fifty-seven-hundred second lieutenants.

Another aspect of Fort Riley's post-war utilization was the creation of the Aggressor School. This school developed, trained, and advised personnel in doctrine and tactics that U.S. enemies might employ in battle.

The Cavalry Replacement Training Center (CRTC), located at Camp Forsyth, trained soldiers in mechanized and mounted warfare during World War II. Pictured here are trainees on a field exercise developing their skills at transporting various types of equipment by horse and mule. The CRTC eventually trained more than 124,000 soldiers during the four years of the war.

The Aggressor School was a hub of activity for a mythical foreign power. Participants wore dark green uniforms identifiable by a combination of colored collar tabs, epaulets, sleeve patches, and crested helmets. They spoke a specially created language—a conglomeration of Spanish, Italian, and French. Once trained, these personnel traveled to other bases around the country to serve as the opposing force in training exercises. The school continued its operation until the summer of 1963.

Beginning in August 1948 the Tenth Infantry Division—one of ten army training divisions—was reactivated at Camp Funston. Under the slogan "Training America's finest young men to be the world's best soldiers," the division trained more than thirteen thousand men in 1949. The following year Fort Riley readied more than fifteen thousand men as overseas replacements. Training intensified with the outbreak of the Korean Conflict in June 1950, and over the next three years thousands of soldiers trained at Fort Riley.

The Army General School (AGS) replaced the Ground General School in January 1950. The AGS mission basically continued that of its predecessor by conducting an officers candidate school, an intelligence school for officers and enlisted men, a counterintelligence school, and the field training aggressor unit. Participants focused on methods of gathering and utilizing combat intelligence and applied lessons from World War II to their core studies.

In early October 1954 the War Department announced that as part of Operation Gyroscope the Tenth Infantry would assume occupation duty in Germany, replacing the First Infantry Division, also known as the Big Red One. The fort welcomed its new tenant in the summer of 1955. The arrival of Big Red One soldiers required construction of additional support facilities. Work began in January 1956 on Custer Hill to build quarters, barracks, and work areas. By the following spring housing units were ready for occupancy.

As part of the Cold War preparedness in the late 1950s, regular army recruits received basic military and advanced individual training from First Infantry Division units before going to Germany. Soldiers and the post conducted reserve and ROTC summer camps as well as army rifle and pistol competitions. They also provided assistance to area communities during adverse weather. The Big Red One left Fort Riley for the first time in the summer of 1965.

To enhance the fort's training capabilities, fifty thousand acres were added to the reservation in 1966. This permitted adequate space for two divisional brigades to train simultaneously. Because the fort's expansion coincided with the completion of Milford Dam in 1967, protests against taking land soured relations with civilian neighbors.

Following nearly five years of combat in Vietnam, the colors of the First Infantry Division returned to Fort Riley in April 1970. They assumed the NATO commitment of the Twenty-Fourth Infantry Division. Over the next two decades, the First Infantry Division took part in additional REFORGERs, training at the National Training Center, and hosting ROTC summer camps. This last function was part of the training conducted by the Third ROTC Region Headquarters, which operated at Fort Riley from 1973 until 1992. The fort also hosted the model U.S. Army Correctional Training Brigade at Camp Funston. This camp experimented retraining and rehabilitating soldiers convicted of minor offenses before their return to active duty or civilian life.

Iraq's aggression against its neighbor Kuwait in the summer of 1990 led to deployment of U.S. forces to the Middle East later that year. This action, known as Operation Desert Shield/Desert Storm, was the largest overseas deployment of American troops since the Vietnam conflict. In November 1990 high command alerted the First Infantry Division

As the United States prepared to enter World War II, soldiers trained in both horse and mechanized warfare. Pictured here is a mounted cavalryman passing a message to a soldier sitting a top an M-8 armored car.

to prepare for deployment to this theater of operations. Over the next two months approximately fourteen thousand soldiers and six thousand pieces of equipment left Fort Riley by air, rail, and sea to the Kuwaiti theater. When hostilities ended in Iraq, troops returned to Fort Riley and resumed their normal teaching and training schedules.

In recent years soldiers from Fort Riley have performed a variety of missions, from fighting forest fires in the Pacific Northwest to overseas duty in the Caribbean and Europe. In early 1993 units were sent on United Nations duty to Somalia. Troops from Fort Riley went to Haiti in January 1996 and to Bosnia in the spring of 1997 in support of peace-keeping and humanitarian missions.

In the fall of 1995 the fort hosted an important effort at international cooperation: Peacekeeper '95. This exercise was the first combined United States–Russian training to occur on American soil. The First Infantry Division and Fort Riley hosted soldiers from Russia's Third Infantry Division and the Twenty-Seventh Guards Motorized Rifle Division. During this two-week mission, units trained for joint operations relating to humanitarian relief and disaster assistance.

In the fall of 1955 the First Infantry Division came to Fort Riley following a decade of occupation duty in Germany. For the next forty years, with the exception of service in Vietnam and the Gulf War of 1991, the Big Red One, as the division was known, was garrisoned at the fort. This 1960 photograph shows elements of the division passing in review as it celebrates the anniversary of its formation.

Downsizing the army in the early 1990s profoundly affected Fort Riley. Both the Third Region ROTC Headquarters and the Correctional Training Brigade closed in 1992. In March 1996 the headquarters of the First Infantry Division moved from Fort Riley to Germany. Troop levels declined from approximately fourteen thousand soldiers at the beginning of the decade to ten thousand in 1997. Today one brigade each from the First Infantry Division and the First Armored Division are located at the fort. The 937th Engineer Group is also assigned to the post along with several tenant activities including MEDDAC (medical services), DENTAC (dental services), and the Southwest Civilian Personnel Office. In June 1999 the headquarters of the Twenty-fourth Infantry Division was reactivated at Fort Riley. These three maneuver brigades came from Georgia and North and South Carolina Army National Guard Units.

During the 1990s efforts have continued to upgrade facilities. Completion of a second multipurpose gunnery complex along with other improvements to the ranges have enabled units to fire any conventional weapon at these sites. New housing units have been built in the Custer Hill area, replacing quarters constructed in the early 1960s. A new water treatment plant serving the entire post was completed in 1992.

Modernization efforts continued with the demolition of World War II buildings in the Camps Forsyth and Funston areas. A new post commissary opened in the Forsyth area in the spring of 1997. Funston became home to reserves and national guard units as well as the defense reutilization and marketing office. In addition, a new railhead was constructed to speed deployment of equipment to ports of debarkation and training exercises. This facility enhanced the fort's power projection image as it nears a new century. These and other improvements are in keeping with a command theme that Fort Riley is today "Home to America's Army." As long as civilian and army leaders continue to recognize the historic adaptability of Fort Riley as a training and deployment center, it will maintain both its usefulness to the nation and its position in the army's force structure.

Throughout its history, Fort Riley's importance has largely corresponded to the ebb and flow of army missions and appropriations. Factors such as its central location, adequate maneuver space, and maintenance of transportation facilities ensured the fort's viability through the years. Following the settlement of the frontier in the 1890s and the end of ongoing Indian struggles, the establishment of a cavalry school of instruction further enhanced the fort's future. Increasingly during the twentieth century the fort's mission has been tied to its educational and training duties. This has been its history since the creation of Camp Center in 1853 and has continued through the years as Fort Riley assembled and prepared troops to confront Indians on the frontier or respond to national emergencies in the Spanish–American War, World War I, World War II, Korea, Vietnam, or Desert Storm. Whether the frontier meant Kansas, the Great Plains, or the world beyond our national borders, Fort Riley has served as sentinel, community, and school.

Appendix

Commanding Officers of Fort Riley, 1853–1890

Captain Charles S. Lovell, Sixth Infantry, May 1853–October 1853

Major Albermarle Cady, Sixth Infantry, October 1853–May 1854

Major William Montgomery, Second Infantry, May 1854–May 1855

Captain Sammuel Woods, Sixth Infantry, May 1855–July 1855

Captain Edmund A. Ogden, Quartermaster Department,
July 1855–August 1855

Captain Washington J. Newton, Second Dragoons,
August 1855–September 1855

Captain Hamilton W. Merrill, Second Dragoons,
September 1855–October 1855, April 1856–May 1856

Lieutenant Colonel Philip St. George Cooke, Second Dragoons,
October 1855–December 1855, January 1856–April 1856,
May 1856–August 1856, November 1856–May 1857

Lieutenant Arthur D. Tree, Second Dragoons,
September 1856–November 1856

Captain Lewis A. Armistead, Sixth Infantry,
May 1857–June 1857, July 1857–November 1857

Captain George H. Stewart, First Cavalry, June 1857–July 1857

Major William Emory, First Cavalry, November 1857–April 1858

Colonel Edwin V. Sumner, First Cavalry, April 1858–June 1858

Major Martin Burke, Second Artillery, June 1858–August 1858

Lieutenant Colonel Joseph E. Johnston, First Cavalry,
August 1858–September 1858

Captain Horace Brooks, Second Artillery,
September 1858–December 1858

Major John Sedgwick, First Cavalry,
December 1858–May 1859, November 1859–May 1860

Captain Horace Brooks, Second Artillery, May 1859–September 1859

Captain Henry W. Wessells, Second Infantry,
September 1859–October 1859, January 1861–October 1861

Captain William D. De Saussure, First Cavalry,
October 1859–November 1859

Captain Nathaniel Lyon, Second Infantry, May 1860–November 1860

Captain Julius Hayden, Second Infantry,
November 1860–January 1861

Captain James W. Graham, First Kansas Home Guard,
October 1861–May 1862

Lieutenant Colonel Owen A. Bassett, Second Kansas Cavalry,
May 1862–June 1862

Captain John E. Stewart, Ninth Kansas Cavalry, June 1862–May 1863

Captain W.N.F. Read, Ninth Kansas Cavalry, May 1863–June 1863

Captain Nick L. Beuter, Twelfth Kansas Infantry, June 1863–July 1863

Captain Edmund G. Ross, Eleventh Kansas Cavalry,
July 1863–August 1863

Captain Nathaniel A. Adams, Eleventh Kansas Cavalry,
August 1863–March 1864

Captain O. Dunlap, Fifteenth Kansas Cavalry, March 1864–May 1864

Captain D.S. Malvern, Seventh Iowa Cavalry, May 1864–August 1864

Captain Henry Booth, Eleventh Kansas Cavalry,
August 1864–November 1864

Lieutenant John A. Edington, Ninth Wisconsin Battery,
November 1864–December 1864

Major Jesse L. Pritchard, Second Colorado Cavalry,
December 1864–February 1865

Captain A.W. Burton, Twelfth Kansas Infantry,
February 1865–March 1865, April 1865–May 1865

Colonel Andrew P. Caraher, Second Infantry, March 1865–April 1865

Colonel Henry E. Maynadier, Fifth U.S. Volunteers,
May 1865–August 1865

Captain Thomas Moses Jr., Second Colorado Cavalry,
August 1865–September 1865

Lieutenant Colonel Josias R. King, Second U.S. Volunteers,
September 1865–October 1865

Captain Robert S. La Motte, Thirteenth Infantry,
October 1865–November 1865

Major William Clinton, Thirteenth Infantry,
November 1865–March 1866

Major J.W. Davidson, Second Cavalry,
March 1866–June 1866, September 1866–November 1866

Captain Henry E. Noyes, Second Cavalry, June 1866–September 1866

Colonel Andrew J. Smith, Seventh Cavalry,
September 1866–December 1867

Lieutenant Colonel George A. Custer, Seventh Cavalry,
December 1866–March 1867

Captain John N. Craig, Thirty-eighth Infantry, March 1867–April 1867

Major Alfred Gibbs, Seventh Cavalry, April 1867–May 1867

Captain Charles C. Parsons, Fourth Artillery, May 1867–July 1867

Brevet Captain Charles Warner, Fourth Artillery, July 1867–August 1867

Colonel Benjamin H. Grierson, Tenth Cavalry, August 1867–April 1868

Colonel William Hoffman, Third Infantry, April 1868–June 1868

Major Thomas C. English, Fifth Infantry, June 1868–May 1869

Major John Hamilton, First Artillery, May 1869–September 1869

Captain William M. Graham, First Artillery, September 1869–May 1871

Captain Adna R. Chaffee, Sixth Cavalry, May 1871–October 1871

Colonel James Oakes, Sixth Cavalry, October 1871–December 1871,
November 1872–December 1872, January 1873–April 1873

Lieutenant Colonel Thomas W. Neill, Sixth Cavalry,
December 1871–May 1872, October 1872–November 1872

Captain Sheldon Sturgeon, Sixth Cavalry, May 1872–June 1872

Lieutenant William M. Wallace, Sixth Cavalry, June 1872, October 1872

Captain Curwin B. McLellan, Sixth Cavalry,
December 1872–January 1873, March 1874–April 1874

Lieutenant Edmund C. Hentig, Sixth Cavalry, April 1873–October 1873

Colonel De Lancey Floyd-Jones, Third Infantry,
October 1873–January 1874, April 1874–July 1874

Major Henry L. Chipman, Third Infantry, January 1874–March 1874

Captain Ezra P. Ewers, Fifth Infantry, July 1874–August 1874

Lieutenant George McDermott, Fifth Infantry,
    August 1874–November 1874

Lieutenant Colonel Joseph N.G. Whistler, Fifth Infantry,
    November 1874–June 1875, July 1876–August 1876

Captain Henry B. Bristol, Fifth Infantry, June 1875–August 1875

Second Lieutenant James A. Payne, Nineteenth Infantry,
    August 1876–October 1876

Captain William Graves, Second Artillery,
    October 1876–November 1876

Captain Joseph T. Haskell, Twenty-third Infantry
    November 1876–January 1877, February 1877–May 1877

Lieutenant Colonel Richard I. Dodge, Twenty-third Infantry,
    January 1877–February 1877, May 1877–June 1877

Colonel Galusha Pennypacker, Sixteenth Infantry,
    June 1877–August 1877, October 1877–November 1877,
    December 1877–February 1878, March 1878–April 1879,
    August 1879–November 1880

Captain Thomas E. Rose, Sixteenth Infantry,
    August 1877–October 1877, November 1877–December 1877,
    February 1878–March 1878, April 1879–July 1879

Major Charles A. Webb, Sixteenth Infantry,
    July 1879–August 1879, November 1880–December 1880

Major Eugene B. Beaumont, Fourth Cavalry,
    December 1880–January 1881, March 1881–May 1881

Captain Edward M. Heyl, Fourth Cavalry, January 1881–March 1881

Lieutenant Alexander W. Patch, Fourth Cavalry,
    May 1881–November 1881

Colonel Edward Patch, Ninth Cavalry, November 1881,
    April 1882–June 1882, July 1882–August 1882,
    October 1882–November 1882, February 1883–September 1883,
    November 1883–May 1884, November 1884–December 1884

Lieutenant Clarence A. Stedman, Ninth Cavalry, November 1881

Lieutenant Eugene D. Dimmick, Ninth Cavalry,
    November 1881–December 1881

Captain John S. Loud, Ninth Cavalry,
    January 1882–February 1882, January 1885

Lieutenant Colonel Nathan A. M. Dudley, Ninth Cavalry,
    February 1882–April 1882, September 1884–October 1884

Captain William R. Maize, Twentieth Infantry,
    June 1882–July 1882, August 1882–October 1882

Major Thomas B. Dewees, Ninth Cavalry, November 1882–January 1883

Captain George A. Purington, Ninth Cavalry,
    January 1883–February 1883

Major Frederick W. Benteen, Ninth Cavalry, October 1883

Captain Francis Moon, Ninth Cavalry, June 1884–July 1884

Captain Louis H. Rucker, Ninth Cavalry, August 1884

Captain John S. McNaught, Twentieth Infantry,
    February 1885–April 1885

Captain Francis Moore, Ninth Cavalry, May 1885

Lieutenant Alfred M. Palmer, Twenty-fourth Infantry,
    June 1885–July 1885

Lieutenant Colonel Charles E. Compton, Fifth Cavalry,
   July 1885–March 1887

Captain Joseph T. Haskell, Twenty-third Infantry, April 1887

Colonel James F. Wade, Fifth Cavalry, May 1887–June 1887

Captain William H. McLaughlin, Eighteenth Infantry, July 1887

Colonel James W. Forsyth, Seventh Cavalry,
   August 1887–December 1887, February 1888–June 1888,
   September 1888–April 1889, October 1889,
   December 1889–June 1890, August 1890–October 1890,
   February 1891–November 1891, January 1892–October 1894

Major Samuel M. Whitside, Seventh Cavalry,
   January 1888, January 1891, December 1891

Major John M. Bacon, Seventh Cavalry, July 1888–August 1888,
   May 1889–August 1889, November 1889, July 1890

Captain Frank C. Grugan, Second Artillery, September 1889

Major E.B. Williston, Third Artillery, November 1890–December 1890

COMMANDING OFFICERS OF FORT RILEY, 1980 TO 2003

Major General Edward Partan, July 1980–December 1982

Major General Neil Creighton, December 1982–June 1984

Major General Ronald L. Watts, July 1984–April 1986

Major General Leonard P. Wishart III, April 1986–July 1988

Major General Gordon R. Sullivan, July 1988–July 1989

Major General Thomas G. Rhame, July 1989–July 1991

Major General William Hartzog, July 1991–June 1993

Major General Josue Robles, June 1993–June 1994

Major General Randolph H. House, July 1994–June 1996

Major General Michael Dodson, June 1996–January 1998

Major General Freddy McFarren, February 1998–August 2000

Major General Robert J. St. Onge, August 2000–November 2001

Major General Thomas F. Metz, November 2001–February 2003

FURTHER READING

Carlson, Paul H. *The Plains Indians*. College Station: Texas A&M Press, 1999.

Castel, Albert. *A Frontier State At War: Kansas, 1861–1865*. Lawrence: Kansas Heritage Press, 1992.

Chalfant, William Y. *Cheyennes and Horse Soldiers: The 1857 Expedition and the Battle of Solomon's Fork*. Norman: University of Oklahoma Press, 1989.

Dobak, William. *Fort Riley and Its Neighbors: Military Money and Economic Growth 1853–1895*. Norman: University of Oklahoma Press, 1998.

Franzen, Susan. *Behind the Facade of Fort Riley's Hometown: The Inside Story of Junction City, Kansas*. Ames, Iowa: Pivot Press, 1998.

Goodrich, Thomas. *War to the Knife: Bleeding Kansas, 1854–1861*. Mechanicsburg, Pa.: Stackpole Books, 1998.

Kennedy, W.J.D. *On the Plains With Custer and Hancock: The Journal of Isaac Coates, Army Surgeon*. Boulder, Colo.: Johnson Books, 1983.

Leckie, William. *The Buffalo Soldiers: A Narrative of the Negro Cavalry in the West*. Norman: University of Oklahoma Press, 1967.

Leckie, William. *The Military Conquest of the Southern Plains*. Norman: University of Oklahoma Press, 1963.

Lowe, Percival G. *Five Years a Dragoon ('49–'54) And Other Adventures on the Great Plains*. Norman: University of Oklahoma Press, 1991.

Powers, Ramon and James N. Leiker. "Cholera Among the Plains Indians: Perceptions, Causes, Consequences." *Western Historical Quarterly* 29 (Autumn 1998): 317–40.

Pride, W.F. *The History of Fort Riley.* Fort Riley, Kans.: United States Cavalry Museum, 1987.

Rickey, Don. *Forty Miles A Day on Beans and Hay: The Enlisted Soldier Fighting the Indian Wars.* Norman: University of Oklahoma Press, 1963.

Sherow, James E. and William S. Reeder Jr. "A Richly Textured Community: Fort Riley, Kansas, and American Indians, 1853–1911." *Kansas History: A Journal of the Central Plains* 21 (Spring 1998): 2–17.

Stallard, Patricia. *Glittering Misery: Dependents of the Indian Fighting Army.* Norman: University of Oklahoma Press, 1992.

Unrau, William E. *White Man's Wicked Water: The Alcohol Trade and Prohibition in Indian Country , 1802–1892.* Lawrence: University Press of Kansas, 1996.

Utley, Robert M., ed. *Life in Custer's Cavalry: Diaries and Letters of Albert and Jennie Barnitz, 1867–1868.* New Haven: Yale University Press, 1977.

Utley, Robert M. *Frontier Regulars: The United States Army and the Indian, 1866–1891.* New York: Macmillan Publishing, 1973.

Utley, Robert M. *Frontiersmen in Blue: The United States Army and the Indian, 1848–1865.* Lincoln: University of Nebraska Press, 1967.

West, Elliott. *The Contested Plains: Indians, Goldseekers, and the Rush to Colorado.* Lawrence: University Press of Kansas, 1998.

Acknowledgments

William McKale wishes to acknowledge Terry Van Meter, director of the U.S. Cavalry Museum, who encouraged and supported this project and my part in it from the outset. Bill Lind, Mike Meier, Deanne Blanton, and Rick Pueser of the Old Military and Civil Textual Reference Branch, National Archives and Records Administration were extremely helpful in directing my efforts and locating records during visits to Washington. Finally, to my wife, Elaine, I thank her for being there and serving as my compass through the research and writing of this monograph.

William Young wishes to thank Bill McKale, whose open and honest interest in history for the general population started him researching this project. I also want to thank my friend and editor Virgil Dean of the Kansas State Historical Society for his careful editing and encouragement. Most of all I thank my wife, Michelle, who patiently watched me assume yet another project, but without complaint helped me commit the time necessary to finish it.

Illustration Credits

All illustrations are from the collections of the Kansas State Historical Society, with the following exceptions: 12–13, 24, 26 U.S. Cavalry Museum, Fort Riley; 36 Clarence P. Hornung Collection; 39 U.S. Cavalry Museum, Fort Riley; 43 U.S. Military Academy Archives; 62, 66, 76, 87, 89 U.S. Cavalry Museum, Fort Riley; 91 Pennell Collection, Kansas Collection, University of Kansas Libraries; 93 U.S. Cavalry Museum, Fort Riley; 95 Pennell Collection; 110, 120, 121, 122 U. S. Cavalry Museum, Fort Riley; 123, 125 Pennell Collection; 129, 131 U.S. Cavalry Museum, Fort Riley.

This publication has been financed in part with federal funds from the National Park Service, a division of the United States Department of the Interior, and administered by the Kansas State Historical Society. The contents and opinions, however, do not necessarily reflect the views or policies of the United States Department of the Interior or the Kansas State Historical Society.

The program receives federal financial assistance. Under Title VI of the Civil Rights Act of 1964, Section 504 of the Rehabilitation Act of 1973, and the Age Discrimination Act of 1975, as amended, the United States Department of the Interior prohibits discrimination on the basis of race, color, national origin, disability, or age in its federally assisted programs. If you believe you have been discriminated against in any program, activity, or facility as described above, or if you desire further information, please write to: Office of Equal Opportunity, National Park Service, P.O. Box 37127, Washington, D.C. 20012-7127.